Reinvent Your
Bathroom

By Christine E. Barnes and the Editors of Sunset Books

MENLO PARK · CALIFORNIA

SUNSET BOOKS

VICE PRESIDENT, GENERAL MANAGER: Richard A. Smeby

VICE PRESIDENT, EDITORIAL DIRECTOR: Bob Doyle

PRODUCTION DIRECTOR: Lory Day

DIRECTOR OPERATIONS: Rosann Sutherland

RETAIL SALES DEVELOPMENT MANAGER: Linda Barker

ART DIRECTOR: Vasken Guiragossian

STAFF FOR THIS BOOK

DEVELOPMENTAL EDITOR: Linda J. Selden

PROJECT DESIGNERS: Melinda D. Douros, Heidi M. Emmett,
D. Kimberly Smith, and Debra S. Weiss

COPY EDITOR AND INDEXER: Julie Harris

PHOTO DIRECTOR/STYLIST: JoAnn Masaoka Van Atta

DESIGN: Dorothy Marschall/Marschall Design

PAGE PRODUCTION: Janie Farn

ILLUSTRATOR: Beverley Bozarth Colgan

PHOTOGRAPHER: E. Andrew McKinney

PRODUCTION COORDINATOR: Eligio Hernandez

PROOFREADER: Mary Roybal

10 9 8 7 6 5 4 3 2 1

First printing April 2003.
Copyright © 2003, Sunset Publishing Corporation,
Menlo Park, CA 94025. First edition. All rights reserved,
including the right of reproduction in whole or in part
in any form.

ISBN 0–376–01795–3
Library of Congress Control Number: 2002115938
Printed in the United States of America.

For additional copies of *Reinvent Your Bathroom* or any
other Sunset book, call 1–800–526–5111 or see our web
site at *www.sunsetbooks.com*.

COVER: Crisp white components lighten and brighten
a small bath; blue vinyl tile and a curtained cupboard
suggest a seaside setting.
PHOTOGRAPHY: E. Andrew McKinney
COVER DESIGN: Vasken Guiragossian
PHOTO DIRECTION: JoAnn Masaoka Van Atta

DESIGN CREDITS

Christine E. Barnes: 33, 61,
94, 96, 102, 106, 139 (top right)

Melinda D. Douros: 10, 20,
36, 70, 73–75, 76, 82, 85, 108

Heidi M. Emmett: 17, 23 (top
right and bottom), 28, 42, 108,
114, 120, 130, 134, 136, 138,
139 (top right)

**D. Kimberly Smith/Deer
Creek Design:** 10, 20, 23 (left),
24, 36, 58, 67, 70, 76, 82, 85, 90,
108, 134

Debra S. Weiss: 14, 28, 50, 54,
61, 98, 102, 106, 108, 126, 139
(bottom)

Woodgrain Woodworks: 20

Are you in the mood to change your bathroom—but not up for a total remodel? If that's the case, your room is a prime candidate for *reinvention*. The reinvent concept is simple: start with the "givens" in your room and add new materials and features as your skill, budget, and schedule allow. If your bathroom is cramped, for example, a lighter wall treatment or a checkerboard-tile floor can make it *feel* more expansive. Storage and decorative details can be part of your theme or can cover up features you don't like.

The bathrooms shown here include projects for walls, floors, countertops, and cabinets, along with quick-and-easy finishing touches. The effects may be dramatic, but the changes are relatively easy to achieve because the steps are simple and the supplies are readily available. Best of all, you get the satisfaction and pleasure that come from personal effort and accomplishment.

Behind each room featured in this book is a team of talented and generous people. We would like to thank the following individuals and businesses for their assistance: Accent Lighting, Bay View Tile, Country Wood Furniture, C. R. Laurence Company, Lou Douros, Robert Emmett, Knight's Paint, Bud Migues, Jay Montgomery, Moule Paint and Glass, Pro Glass, Ramey Tile, Sierra Plumbing, Sierra Tile & Stone, Curt Smith, Woodgrain Woodworks, and Young's Carpet One.

A special thanks to the homeowners who invited us into their homes: Barbara and David Sidebottom and Wendy and Martin Weiss.

Contents

Room for Renewal

No other room in the home is more personal and practical than the bathroom. It's the place where you gear up for—and unwind after—each day, and where surfaces

must be moisture-proof and durable. Is it any wonder that the bathroom, next to the kitchen, is the most redone of all spaces in the house? Ꮬ

Country Spa soothes the senses in this everyday getaway

Reinventing your bathroom is easier than ever, thanks to an abundance of affordable, homeowner-friendly materials and doable projects. At the top of everyone's list is tile—on shower walls, vanity

countertops, and floors. You can even tile around a window casing for a custom touch. Paint has the power to dramatically alter the look of a room,

Serene Style emanates from this tranquil space

especially when combined with tissue paper, joint compound, or glazing medium for one-of-a-kind effects. Other time-honored materials for the bathroom include wallpaper and sheet vinyl flooring. Ꮬ When it comes to creating more storage or

giving a room better "bones," wood is the tradi-

Nantucket Charm is trim and tidy, crisp and cool

tional favorite. On the following

pages you'll find instructions for woodworking projects as varied as installing beadboard paneling and molding over drywall and turning a standard bookcase into a storage cupboard. You can also update existing cabinetry by refinishing it with liming wax. A vanity fashioned from a potting bench, a wood screen with cast-iron grille insets, and a corbeled mantel mounted over a tub are

Down-to-earth materials reflect a **Natural Bent**

among the more fanciful designs. ◌ A number of features in this book ensure success: A colored tab at the start of each project tells you the approximate time commitment, such as "Do It Today" or "In a Weekend"; longer projects are identified as "Makeover Magic."

Blues and greens make a **Color Splash**

Simple instructions, photographs, and illustrations guide you through the step-by-step process; tips sprinkled throughout keep you on track. At the end of each chapter, you'll see the "Fresh Ideas" that make each bath special. ◌ Ready to reinvent your bathroom? Soak up the ideas, gather the appropriate tools and materials, and take the plunge!

Tumbled stone surfaces have **Classic Appeal**

Country Spa

AWASH IN PRETTY COLORS and graceful patterns, this reinvented bath typifies the casual spirit of new-country style. Fresh yellow paint brightens the space and makes existing tile look whiter. Wood features—a corbeled mantel for display and a folding screen for privacy— contribute architectural interest, while plants and fabrics soften the edges. Oak cabinetry refinished with liming wax enhances the room's light-and-airy look. A painted urn, banded towels, and a bath bolster add a touch of easygoing elegance to the scheme.

BEFORE: Although the oak cabinets and white tile with blue-gray grout were in good condition, this master bathroom was not living up to its potential.

Corbeled Mantel

A SIMPLE SHELF SUPPORTED BY decorative wood corbels adds depth and interest to the spacious wall above the tub. If the shelf you purchase has a rounded front edge, orient it so the rounded part is on the lower front edge. Corbels come in all sizes and shapes; for this project, select ones that are deep enough to support a 12-inch shelf. The corbels shown here are 8 inches deep.

FINISHED SIZE

approximately

48 inches wide,

12 inches deep,

14 inches tall

MATERIALS

Two corbels,
each approximately
3½ by 13 by 8 inches,
available at home
centers and through
woodworking catalogs
(see Resources, page 142)

8 feet of ⅝-inch
half-round molding

2½-inch paintbrush

Latex primer

Miter box with backsaw

Preprimed MDF shelf,
1 by 12 by 48 inches

Wood glue

Brad nailer with
⅝-inch nails

Spackling

200-grit sandpaper

White latex paint

Stud finder

Steel tape measure

Carpenter's level

Electric driver/drill
with bits*

Four #8 zinc-plated
anchors for drywall,
with screws
(see Step 11)

*When predrilling the
anchor holes, use a bit
with the same diameter
as the anchor "paddle."

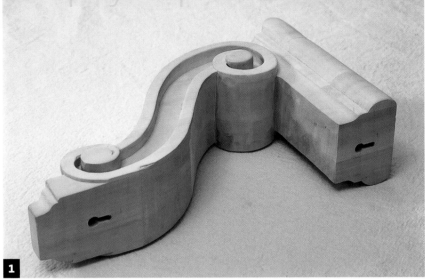

1

Preparing the Corbels and the Molding

1 To ensure that the corbels hang at the same height and the shelf is level, the placement of the mortises (slots) on the back of each corbel must be identical. For best results, take the corbels to a cabinet shop and have them cut as shown above. If you are experienced with a router, you can cut the mortises yourself, but keep in mind that the shape of the corbels makes them difficult to secure for cutting.

2 Prime the corbels and the molding using the 2½-inch brush and the latex primer.

Attaching the Molding

3 Using the miter box with backsaw, cut the molding as follows: Cut one piece several inches longer than needed to fit one side of the shelf; miter one end. Cut the front piece several inches longer than needed to fit; miter one end. Fit the mitered ends together at one front corner of the shelf.

4 Have a helper hold the pieces in place while you mark the other end of the front piece. Miter the end.

5 Miter one end of the remaining side piece.

3

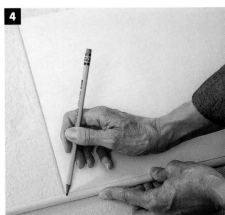

4

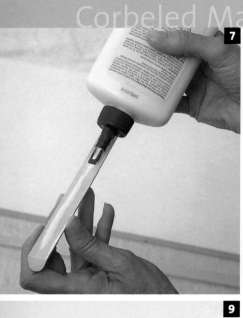

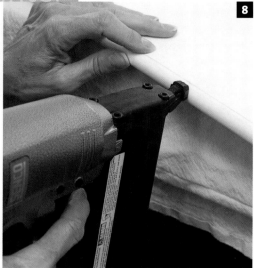

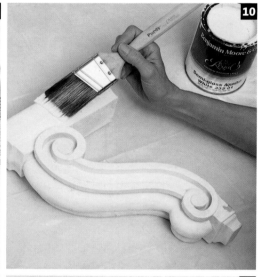

6 After making sure the miters fit nicely at the front corners, mark the remaining ends of the side pieces flush with the back of the shelf; cut off the excess length.

7 Apply a thin bead of wood glue to the wrong side of each molding piece. Attach one side piece to the shelf, followed by the front piece and the remaining side piece.

8 Using the brad nailer and the ⁵⁄₈-inch nails, secure the pieces to the shelf at the ends and every 8 inches.

9 Fill the nail holes and any gaps along the edges and at the corners with spackling. Allow to dry; sand using the 200-grit sandpaper.

Painting the Corbels and the Shelf

10 Paint the corbels and the shelf with the white latex paint and the 2½-inch brush.

Mounting the Shelf

11 Using a stud finder, locate the studs in your wall. The following steps explain how to install hanging hardware into drywall. If the desired placement of a corbel is over a stud, use wood screws instead of anchors and screws.

12 With the aid of a helper, hold the corbels against the wall at the desired height and spacing. (These corbels are spaced 38 inches apart, measuring from center to center.) Use the carpenter's level to make sure they're level. Lightly mark the wall at the upper edge of each corbel.

13 Measure from the upper edge of one corbel to the top of its upper mortise. Measure and mark this distance on the wall, down from the mark you just made, to determine the anchor placement.

14 Drill a pilot hole for the upper anchor.

15 Install the anchor, being careful to screw straight into the wall, not at an angle.

16 Install a screw in the anchor, leaving the shank exposed a distance equal to the depth of the mortise. (Experiment with the corbel, placing it over the screw, until you determine the proper distance.)

17 Use the level to mark the exact location of the upper anchor for the second corbel as follows: Place one end of the level precisely over the *center* of the screw you just installed. Adjust the other end until level; mark the wall for the second anchor. Install the anchor and screw.

18 Measure the distance between the mortises on the first corbel, from top to top.

19 Measure and mark this distance on the wall, down from the center of the first screw.

20 Use the level to ensure that the mark is plumb with the upper screw. Install the lower anchor and screw. Repeat for the second corbel.

21 Hang the two corbels from the screws.

22 Center the shelf on the corbels. Use the brad nailer and the 5/8-inch nails to secure the shelf to the corbels from above. Fill the nail holes with spackling. Allow to dry; sand. Touch up with the paint.

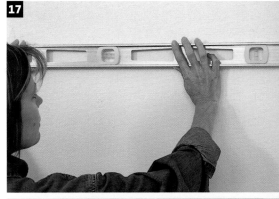

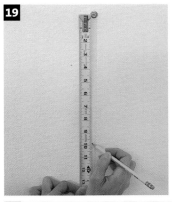

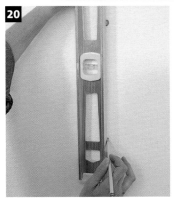

MATERIALS

Plastic sheeting

Electric driver/drill with bits for screws

Brown paper bag for templates

Scissors

Repositionable spray adhesive

Drawer pulls and knobs, with screws

Metal ruler

Awl

150-grit sandpaper

Rubber or latex gloves

Mineral spirits

Lint-free cotton cloths

Wire brush

Liming wax (see Resources, page 142)

Clear furniture finishing wax (see Resources, page 142)

IN A WEEKEND

Liming-Wax Cabinets

LIMING WAX IS A 200-YEAR-OLD TREATMENT used to lift color from wood cabinets, producing a white-grained finish. The wax contains solvents, so remove the doors and drawers and wax them outside; when you work on the cabinet shells, open the windows and set up a fan to blow the fumes away from you. This project involved installation of hardware on oak cabinets that previously had none; disregard Steps 3 through 8 if you're reusing existing hardware or replacing it with same-size new hardware.

Marking for Hardware

1 Cover your work surface with plastic sheeting.

2 Remove conventional hinges. It's not necessary to remove European (hidden) hinges; simply release the hinges inside to remove the doors.

3 Using the paper bag, make a template the size of the raised panel on an upper drawer. Fold the template in half both ways to find the center point; mark. You'll use this point as a guideline for positioning drawer pulls. Spray the back of the template with repositionable adhesive and adhere it to a raised panel.

4 On the back of a drawer pull, measure the distance between screw holes from center to center. Working from the center point on the template, measure and mark the screw hole positions with a pencil.

5 Test your template by marking and drilling the holes on a scrap of wood, then checking to see that a drawer pull fits.

6 Position the template on each drawer and mark the screw hole positions with the awl, pushing it into the wood. When working on a lower, deeper drawer, adhere the template at the upper edge of the raised panel. If you're installing *knobs* on the drawer fronts, mark the positions through the center point. Drill holes at the marks.

7 Placement of knobs on cabinet doors is a matter of taste. To mark the position, make an L-shaped template to fit the raised edge of a door. Spray the back with the adhesive, adhere it, and mark the screw hole position with a pencil.

8 Using the template and the awl, mark each door. The door shown in photo 7 on the previous page is a left-hand door. For each right-hand door, be sure to turn the template over. Drill holes at the marks.

Waxing the Drawers and the Doors

Test Steps 9 through 11 on an inconspicuous area, such as the inside of a door, to determine how much sanding and wire-brushing are required to achieve the look and texture you like.

9 Sand the drawer fronts and both sides of the doors with the 150-grit sandpaper; also sand the drawer and door edges. Wearing gloves, clean the surfaces with mineral spirits and a lint-free cotton cloth.

10 Use the wire brush to "open" the wood pores, brushing in the direction of the grain only. Hold the door or the drawer up to the light periodically to make sure you are opening the pores consistently across the surface of the wood.

11 Wearing gloves, apply the liming wax with a lint-free cloth in circular, overlapping strokes, working it into the grain, until the surface is covered. Wipe away the excess with another lint-free cloth, allowing some wax to remain in the pores. If streaking occurs, apply a little more wax to dissolve the excess; wipe quickly, before the solvent in the wax evaporates. If necessary, use mineral spirits to lift excess wax.

12 Allow the wax to dry 3 to 5 minutes. Buff the surface in the direction of the grain using a lint-free cloth.

13 The next day, apply two coats of clear furniture finishing wax to give the cabinets a more durable finish; buff (see the tip below).

Attaching the Hardware

14 Screw the pulls to the drawers and the knobs to the doors. Insert the drawers into the cabinets and rehang the doors.

TIP

IN A VERY WET AREA, SUCH AS A CHILDREN'S BATH, APPLY TWO COATS OF CLEAR VARNISH OVER THE WAX (SANDING BETWEEN COATS) TO PROTECT THE FINISH.

MATERIALS

Sewing tape measure

Floral fabric,
54 inches wide*

Blue-and-white
seersucker,
54 inches wide*

White bath towel

Batting*

Fabric scissors

Thread

4 yards of ribbon,
1¼ inches wide

Hand-sewing needle

Pins

Lightweight twine
or string

Bead fringe, equal
in length to twice the
ottoman perimeter,
plus ⅛ yard

*See Steps 1–3
for yardage. Buy extra
seersucker if you wish to
embellish towels or
make a bath bolster.

DO IT TODAY

Ottoman Slipcover

A SIMPLE-TO-SEW SLIPCOVER, topped with a reversible cushion, transforms a yard-sale ottoman, adding country color and pattern to the room. An easy technique for gathering fabric makes quick work of sewing the slipcover skirt; bead fringe finishes the hem. The flip side of the seersucker cushion was cut from a white bath towel. Satin-and-sheer ribbons hold the cushion in place.

7

8

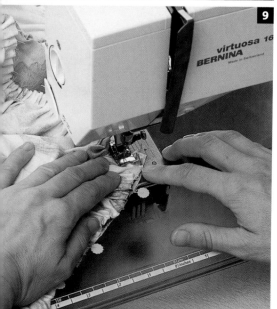

9

Determining Yardage

1 For the slipcover top, measure the width and the length of the ottoman top; add ½ inch to *each* edge for seam allowances.

2 For the slipcover skirt, measure the height of the ottoman from the upper edge to the floor. Add 2 inches to arrive at the cut length of the skirt pieces. For the width, multiply the perimeter of the ottoman by 2 for fullness; divide by 54 (the width of the fabric) to determine the number of skirt pieces needed. Sketch the top and skirt pieces, noting the measurements and adding them up to determine the total yards of floral fabric needed.

3 For the cushion, you'll need enough seersucker, towel, and batting to cut pieces equal in size to the slipcover top piece.

Cutting Out the Pieces

4 From the floral fabric, cut the slipcover top and skirt pieces. Trim the selvages. Join the ends of the skirt pieces using a ½-inch seam allowance to make a loop of fabric. Press the seams open.

5 Cut the seersucker, towel, and batting pieces for the cushion.

Making the Slipcover

6 Cut the ribbon into eight pieces, each 18 inches long. Gather one end of a ribbon piece using the hand-sewing needle and thread. With the seersucker piece right side up, pin and baste the gathered end of the ribbon to a corner of the fabric. Repeat to attach ribbons on the remaining corners. Attach ribbons to the right side of the slipcover top in the same way.

7 Lay the skirt loop right side up. Starting away from a seam allowance (to avoid the bulk), place the twine ³/8 inch from the raw edge. Using the longest and widest zigzag stitch on your machine, zigzag over the twine, being careful not to catch it in the stitching.

8 Making sure the ends of the twine don't slip out of the zigzag stitching, push the fabric along the twine to gather the skirt loop. Right sides together and raw edges aligned, pin the skirt loop to the top piece, distributing the gathers evenly. (Do not catch the free ends of the ribbon in the pinning.) Stitch from the skirt side using a straight stitch and a ½-inch seam allowance, removing the pins before you reach them.

9 As you come to the first corner, pivot and take one diagonal stitch across the corner to avoid creating an exaggerated point. Continue stitching, pivoting at each corner, until you reach the starting point; backstitch to secure.

10 Press the seam allowances up, toward the top piece, being careful not to crush the gathers.

11 Place the slipcover on the ottoman, adjusting the skirt so it hangs evenly on all sides. Place the ottoman where it will sit. Turn up a section of the skirt to the wrong side and pin the bead fringe to it, experimenting with the hem allowance and the fringe placement until the fringe does not drag on the floor; measure the hem allowance. Remove the slipcover.

12 Remove the pins. Turn up the hem allowance to the wrong side and press. Turn in the raw edge to meet the pressed fold; pin. Machine-stitch close to the pinned fold.

13 Pin the bead fringe to the wrong side of the hem. Using a medium-length or longer stitch, sew the fringe to the hem, stitching through all layers.

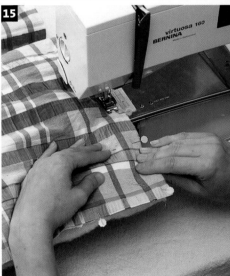

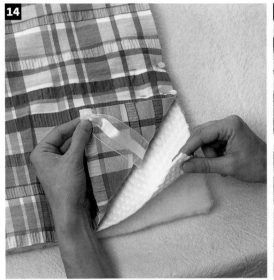

Making the Cushion

14 Layer the cushion pieces with the batting on the bottom, followed by the towel, then the seersucker (right side down). Make sure the free ends of the ribbons are toward the center. Pin the edges, leaving a generous opening on one side for turning the cushion right side out.

15 Stitch around the edges, through all layers, using a ½-inch seam allowance and pivoting at the corners as you did on the slipcover. Trim the seam allowance on the batting only.

16 Turn the cushion right side out and slipstitch the opening closed. Place the slipcover on the ottoman and set the cushion on top. Tie the ribbons at the corners.

MATERIALS

Three wood frames
(see opposite)

Steel tape measure

Circular saw

4- by 8-foot sheet of
½-inch plywood

Three cast-iron grilles,
each 8 by 31 inches
(see Resources, page 142)

Electric driver/drill
with bits

Jigsaw

Wood rasp

Small paintbrush

Latex primer

White latex paint

48 feet of preprimed
chair rail molding,
1¾ by ¹¹⁄₁₆ inches,
to frame grilles

Compound miter saw or
miter box with backsaw

Wood glue

Brad nailer with
1-inch nails

Twenty-four #6 flathead
wood screws, 1 inch long

40 feet of cap molding,
⁹⁄₁₆ by 1⅛ inches,
to trim plywood panels
on the back

2½-inch paintbrush

180-grit sandpaper

Four 1- by 2-inch
hinges, with screws

WOOD SHOP

Ivy Screen

CAST-IRON GRILLES in a twining ivy design are a fresh departure from the gathered fabric panels typically seen in folding screens. The grilles and plywood panels in this screen were sized to fit the custom wood frames illustrated on the facing page; you'll need to adjust the measurements if you work with ready-made frames. Note that this screen will not fold up compactly because of the molding around the grille edges.

FINISHED SIZE three panels, each 18 by 54 inches

18"

1½"

1½"

54"

3"

6"

Custom Frames

The finished dimensions for one of the wood frames are shown at left. If your woodworking skills are limited, have the three frames made by a cabinet or woodworking shop. Ready-made frames are available at unfinished wood furniture stores and large craft stores and through home decorating catalogs.

Preparing the Plywood Pieces

1 Measure the opening on one frame, using the steel tape. (On these frames, the openings are 15 by 40½ inches.)

2 Using the circular saw, cut the ½-inch plywood into three pieces, each ¾ inch larger than the opening *on each edge.* (These pieces were cut to 16½ by 42 inches.) The directions

that follow are for one panel; repeat to make all three panels.

3 Carefully center a grille on a plywood piece. Mark the plywood at the edges of the grille; connect the marks to create cutting lines.

4 Drill a pilot hole through the plywood as shown. Using the jigsaw, cut on the lines.

5 Slip the grille into the just-cut opening on the plywood. If it does not fit, file the edges of the plywood as needed with the rasp. Remove the grille and set it aside.

6 Using the small paintbrush, prime the inside edges of the plywood opening with the latex primer; allow to dry. Paint with the white latex paint; allow to dry. Slip the grille back into the opening.

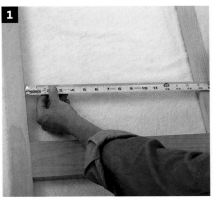

Attaching the Molding

7 Turn the pieces of chair rail molding wrong side up and prime the inner edges. Allow to dry.

8 Set the first piece of chair rail molding so the primed underside edge is along one long edge of the opening. Have the molding overlap the grille ½ inch to cover the irregularities in the metal edges.

9 Mark the ends of the piece for miter cuts, allowing for the ½-inch overlap of the adjoining pieces. (In the photo at top left, the tape measure hangs over the adjoining edge by ½ inch, showing where to mark the miter cut.)

10 Cut the piece using the compound miter saw or the miter box with backsaw. Mark and cut the remaining pieces.

11 Fit the pieces together, checking to see that the molding on opposite sides is equidistant from the plywood's outer edges; adjust if necessary. Have a helper hold the pieces in place while you draw around the outer edges of the molding to create placement guidelines for gluing and nailing.

12 One by one, glue the molding pieces to the plywood edges.

13 Using the brad nailer and 1-inch nails, attach the molding at the ends and every 8 inches. Attach chair molding on the other side.

Finishing the Screen

14 Center the plywood panel over the opening in the wood frame, making sure the plywood extends ¾ inch beyond each edge. Using the electric driver/drill, predrill holes for the #6 wood screws through the plywood and into the frame, placing one hole at each corner and one hole at the midpoint of each side, close to the edges. Install the screws.

15 Mark, cut, glue, and brad-nail the cap molding to cover the screws and the edges of the plywood.

16 Prime the entire panel with the latex primer; allow to dry. Lightly sand the wood with the 180-grit sandpaper. Paint the panel and the grille with the latex paint.

17 Attach the hinges.

Sweet & Simple

Tailored Towels

ABOVE: **White waffleweave towels trimmed with leftover seersucker coordinate with the ottoman.**

Bath Bolster

BELOW: **Leftover slipcover fabrics and ribbon combine to make this little bolster. The form is nothing more than a piece of batting rolled up and held together with a bead of hot glue.**

Painted Urn

ABOVE: **A new resin urn takes on the look of weathered stone when sponged with a mixture of dark acrylic paints and gesso, the pastelike substance used to prime art canvas.**

Picture-frame Tray

Brass handles turn an unfinished wood frame, painted white to match the corbeled mantel and the ivy screen, into a simple tray. Under the glass, handmade paper with wildflowers pressed into the surface is in keeping with the new-country theme.

Graceful Shades

ABOVE: **Milky glass shades in a gentle swirling design soften the existing light fixture and reiterate other white elements in the room.**

Wood Appliqués

BELOW: **Glazed with a mixture of white and yellow paint, wood appliqués lend subtle dimension to the wall above the tub (see Resources, page 142).**

Brightwork

ABOVE: **New brass faucets update the vanity area and echo the curves in the light fixture.**

Serene Style

MONOCHROMATIC COLOR soothes and refreshes both mind and body in this dramatic transformation. Wallpaper with stylized, widely spaced leaves lightens the small rooms and makes them feel larger. Storage boxes mounted on the far wall draw the eye inward, yet maintain the sense of simplicity. A walk-in shower (see page 46) tiled in white marble and smoky green granite makes best use of the space. Among the finishing touches are a bath mat fashioned from an oversize towel and a collage wastebasket decorated with wallpaper leftovers.

BEFORE: Dark, busy wallpaper made the windowless vanity area of this master bath feel small and confining. A dated fixture cast harsh light.

MATERIALS

Portable table, plastic sheeting, and canvas drop cloth (see the tip at right)

Trisodium phosphate or ammonia

Latex primer/sealer*

Brushes, rollers, and roller covers*

Step stool or ladder

Steel tape measure

4-foot carpenter's level

6-foot metal straightedge

Prepasted wallpaper (see Resources, page 142)

24-inch carpenter's square

Scissors

Paint roller with foam roller cover

Paint tray with liner

Wallpaper activator

Medium or large plastic garbage bag

Smoothing brush

Wallpaper sponge

Single-edge razor knife

Broad knife

Wallpaper smoother

Seam roller

*See Step 1.

IN A WEEKEND

Wallpaper

A MINIMALIST PATTERN provides a soft, subtle backdrop for the elegant marble and granite tile in this bath. Specialized tools make the task of hanging wallpaper easier, but patience is perhaps the biggest component of success. Wallpaper activator, rolled on the wrong side of the paper, takes the place of water; it also increases the "open time" of the wet paper, allowing you to work longer with each piece.

Preparing the Walls

1 Remove existing wall coverings and wash off any residue with trisodium phosphate or ammonia and water. Repair any surface defect or it will show through the wallpaper. If your walls are painted with latex paint or if they are new drywall, prime with a latex primer/sealer. Have it tinted to match the wallpaper's background color.

Measuring and Marking the First Wall

2 You can start papering at the midpoint of a wall, in a corner behind a door, or at a focal point in the room. Here, the first strip was hung at the midpoint of the wall that separates the vanity and shower areas. The wall was measured and marked at the midpoint, as shown. The wall was then marked to the *left* of the midpoint a distance equal to half the wallpaper width; this point became the starting point for the first strip.

3 Using the carpenter's level, mark a vertical plumb line at the starting point to create a placement guide for the edge of the first strip. (Never rely on wall edges or door casings to mark a vertical line; these edges are rarely plumb.) Continue the line down the wall using the 6-foot straightedge and the level to keep the line plumb.

4 Measure the height of the wall along the plumb line, from the ceiling to the top of the baseboard, using the steel tape.

Marking and Cutting the First Strip

5 For a professional look, the wallpaper strips should be cut so that the pattern motifs align at the ceiling line around the room. On the wallpaper roll, find the point in the pattern that you want to start at the ceiling. With the carpenter's square, measure 2 inches *above* that point and mark a cutting line across the paper.

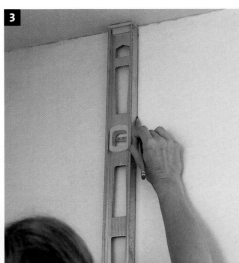

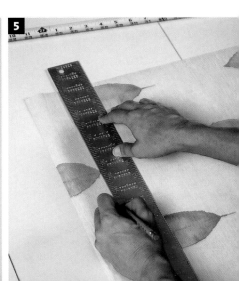

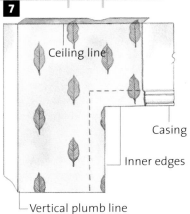

7

Ceiling line

Casing

Inner edges

Vertical plumb line

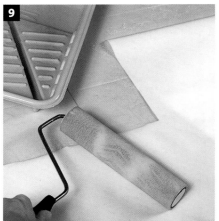

9

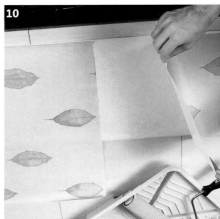

10

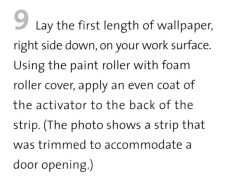

11

12

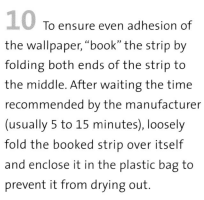

15

6 From the pattern starting point, *not the cutting line,* measure and mark a strip that's equal to the wall height plus 2 inches. Double-check to see that you have 2 inches above and 2 inches below the wall-height measurement. Using the scissors, cut the strip on the marked lines.

7 If your first strip does not require trimming to accommodate a door opening, skip to Step 8. If it does, measure the distance from the vertical plumb line marked in Step 3 across to the inner edge of the side casing. (See the illustration above.) Measure the distance from the ceiling line down to the inner edge of the top casing. Measure, mark, and trim the strip to these measurements.

Hanging the First Strip

8 For safety, turn off the power to the room at the circuit breaker or fuse box. Remove the switch plates and receptacle covers.

9 Lay the first length of wallpaper, right side down, on your work surface. Using the paint roller with foam roller cover, apply an even coat of the activator to the back of the strip. (The photo shows a strip that was trimmed to accommodate a door opening.)

10 To ensure even adhesion of the wallpaper, "book" the strip by folding both ends of the strip to the middle. After waiting the time recommended by the manufacturer (usually 5 to 15 minutes), loosely fold the booked strip over itself and enclose it in the plastic bag to prevent it from drying out.

11 Unfold the top portion of the strip; allow the rest of the strip to drop down. Holding the strip by its upper corners, carefully align the left edge of the strip with the plumb line and align the pattern starting point with the ceiling line.

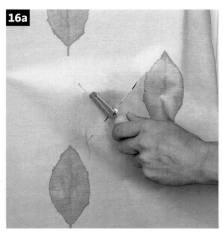

12 Use the smoothing brush to adhere the paper at the ceiling line and to coax out any air bubbles. Wet the wallpaper sponge and wring it nearly dry. Lightly wipe away excess activator at the ceiling. Be gentle with the brush and the sponge; wet wallpaper is fragile.

13 Working from the top down, adhere the paper to the wall as follows: With one hand, align the edge of the strip with the marked line, being careful not to stretch the edge. With your other hand, smooth the paper, spreading your fingers broadly for even pressure.

14 Once the strip is adhered, use the smoothing brush to coax out any air bubbles. Wipe away the excess activator at the edges with the wallpaper sponge. Allow the wallpaper to "rest" for several minutes.

15 Use the scissors to cut a diagonal slit to the outer corner on a door casing, as shown.

16 Using the single-edge razor knife, slit an X in the wallpaper over any light switch or receptacle. Carefully fold back the cut pieces and trim them even with the edges of the opening.

17 Holding down the wallpaper with the broad knife, use the razor knife to trim the excess paper flush with the edge of the side casing. To avoid tearing the wallpaper when you're trimming it, make continuous cuts, keeping the razor blade in contact with the paper while you move the broad knife.

18 Trim the paper above the top casing in the same way. Wait 15 minutes, then use the wallpaper smoother held at a 30-degree angle to smooth the surface of the paper.

19 Trim the excess paper at the ceiling line.

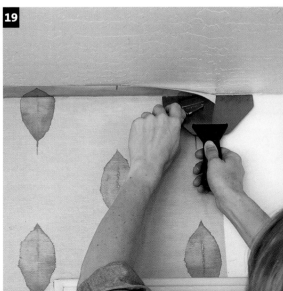

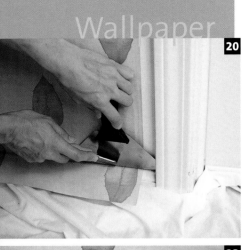

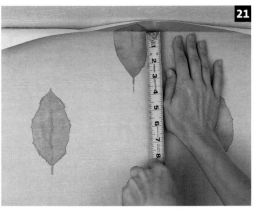

23 Where the first and second strips meet, adhere the edges with the seam roller. Use a light touch to avoid squeezing too much adhesive from under the seam. Continue hanging strips in the same manner.

Turning the Corner

24 When you approach a corner, measure from the edge of the most recent strip to the corner in three places; add ¼ inch to the largest measurement. Mark and trim a new wallpaper strip to this width to allow the paper to turn the corner. Set aside the leftover piece.

25 Hang the strip. Smooth it with the brush and wipe it with the sponge. Snip the ¼ inch at the ceiling line and at the baseboard to make the strip fit around the corner.

26 Measure the width of the leftover piece. Starting in the corner, measure and mark that distance on the adjoining wall. Using the level and the straightedge, mark a plumb line down the length of the wall.

27 Hang the piece, aligning one edge of the strip with the plumb line and butting the other edge into the corner.

28 Continue hanging wallpaper strips around the room, trimming the final one to butt against the starting plumb line.

20 Trim the excess paper at the baseboard.

Hanging Subsequent Strips

21 Measure, mark, and cut the next strip. (In this case, the second strip is short because it falls above the door.) Adhere the strip at the ceiling line. If necessary, measure a motif to make sure the pattern is properly positioned.

22 Work the strip down the wall, aligning its edge with the edge of the first strip. Smooth, sponge, and trim as you did the first strip. Change the razor blade often.

MATERIALS

Fabric scissors

Bath sheet,
approximately
32 by 52 inches

Dinner plate

Flower-head pins,
available at fabric stores
and quilt shops*

1 yard of striped home
decorating fabric,
54 inches wide

6- by 24-inch acrylic
rotary ruler, available
at fabric stores and
quilt shops

Rotary cutting mat
(optional)

Thread

*These pins, which have
flat heads and long
shanks, distort thick fabrics
less than standard pins.

DO IT TODAY

Bath Mat

A MAT SEWN FROM A SINGLE BATH SHEET (an oversize bath towel) adds a touch of softness underfoot. For easier sewing, choose a bath sheet that is not too plush. Bias binding cut from a striped fabric finishes the edge in crisp style. Be sure to prewash both fabrics so you can launder the mat without shrinkage.

FINISHED SIZE approximately 20 by 30 inches

TIP

A WALKING-FOOT ATTACH-

MENT FOR YOUR SEWING

MACHINE MAKES EASY

WORK OF SEWING LAYERS

OF THICK TERRY CLOTH.

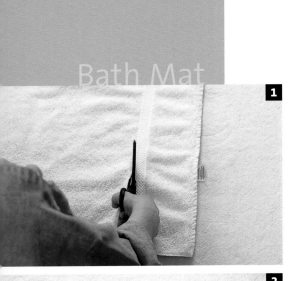

Preparing the Bath Sheet

1 With the fabric scissors, carefully cut off each end of the bath sheet just above the woven band.

2 Fold the bath sheet in half cross-wise, aligning the cut edges and the side edges precisely. Using the plate, mark a curve at each corner.

3 Carefully pin the layers together at the edges, following the curves at the corners as shown.

Making the Bias Binding

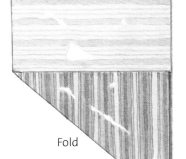

4 Fold one end of the striped fabric at a 45-degree angle as shown; press the fold. Cut on the fold. Set the triangular piece aside.

5 Using the rotary ruler, measure and mark 3-inch-wide bias strips parallel to the just-cut edge. Mark enough strips to encircle the folded bath sheet, plus 18 inches. Cut the strips.

6 Trim the selvages from the ends of the strips. With right sides together, overlap the ends of two strips as shown below; pin. Stitch using a ¼-inch seam allowance and your regular presser foot; press the seam allowances open. Repeat with the remaining strips to make one long binding strip.

TIP

REMOVE EACH PIN AS YOU APPROACH IT. SEWING OVER PINS CAN BREAK THE NEEDLE AND DAMAGE YOUR MACHINE.

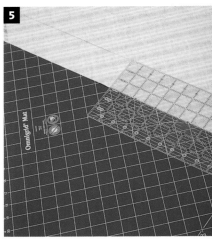

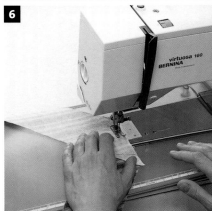

Selvage

Selvage

Fold

Cut edge

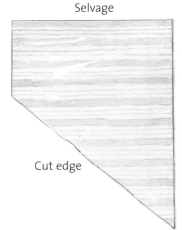

7

Fold

Fold

Hanging Loop

9

7 From the binding strip, cut a 6-inch-long strip for the hanging loop. Trim it to 2 inches wide. Fold the strip in half lengthwise, wrong sides together, and press. Open up the strip and fold the raw edges in to meet the pressed fold, as shown; refold the strip lengthwise and re-press. Set the hanging loop aside.

Attaching the Binding

8 Fold under one angled end of the long binding strip ¼ inch to the wrong side and press. Fold the strip in half lengthwise, wrong sides together, and press.

9 Starting on either long edge of the folded bath sheet, carefully remove the pins, align the raw edges of the long folded binding strip with the raw edges of the bath sheet, and pin through all layers. (Be sure the raw edges of the bath sheet and the strip stay precisely aligned.) At the corners, align the raw edges of the strip with the marked curves; coax the strip around

the curves, being careful not to stretch it. At the midpoint on either short edge, fold the hanging loop as shown above right and pin it to the bath sheet before pinning the binding strip.

10 Attach the walking foot and set your machine for the longest stitch. Leaving 3 inches of the binding strip free, stitch the strip to the bath sheet using a ¼-inch seam allowance.

11 When you reach the starting point, trim the finishing end at an angle and tuck it into the starting end of the strip. Finish stitching the strip to the bath sheet.

12 Trim the marked curves on the bath sheet flush with the raw edges of the strip.

13 Turn the mat over. Bring the binding to the front, just covering the previous stitching with the folded edge; pin. Stitch close to the fold, through all thicknesses.

10

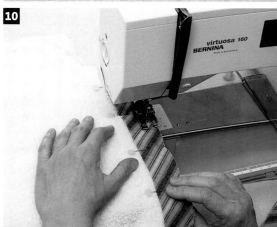

11

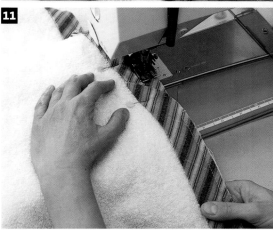

13

MATERIALS

Table saw

Three 1-by-8 pieces of
lumber, each 8 feet long

Three wood picture frames

Steel tape measure

2-inch paintbrush

Latex primer

Latex paint

Wood glue

Brad nailer with
1½- and ¾-inch nails

Spackling

180-grit sandpaper

Six 1¾-inch-long keyhole
screwplates, with screws

Small combination square

Fence*

Two clamps

Router with two-flute,
straight, ½-inch router bit

Electric driver/drill
with bits

Large sheets of paper

Two pushpins

Carpenter's level

Awl (optional)

Six #6 nylon anchors
for drywall, with #6
roundhead screws, 1½
inches long

*See "Using a Fence," page 39.

IN A WEEKEND

Picture-frame Boxes

OPEN BACKS ON THESE FRAMED BOXES direct the eye to the wallpaper's graceful pattern, making the boxes all but disappear into the wall. Picture frames and 1-by-8 lumber are the raw materials needed to construct these storage units. You have lots of options in picture-frame sizes and shapes, as well as styles. Screwplates recessed in the back edges allow the boxes to mount flat against the wall; if you don't have a router, ask a cabinet shop to cut the recesses for you.

FINISHED SIZE 11 by 14 inches, 16 by 20 inches, and 7 by 29 inches; approximately 8 inches deep

TIP

THE HARDWARE FOR HANGING
THE BOXES IS ESSENTIAL TO
THIS PROJECT. SCREWPLATES
(AT TOP) ATTACHED TO THE
BACK EDGES HAVE PRECISE
OPENINGS FOR THE HEADS
OF THE HANGING SCREWS.
NYLON ANCHORS (AT BOTTOM)
INSERTED IN THE DRYWALL
PROVIDE EXTRA SUPPORT FOR
THE HANGING SCREWS.

Constructing the Boxes

Steps for making one box follow, but it's most efficient to make all the boxes at once.

1 Cut one 1-by-8 the same length as the longest side of the longest picture frame. Position the frame upside down on your work surface. Place the 1-by-8 piece, on its edge, on the top or bottom of the frame, aligning the inner edge of the lumber with the inner edge of the frame. Mark a line on the frame along the *outer* edge of the lumber. Repeat on the opposite side. See the illustration at right.

2 Place the 1-by-8 piece on one of the sides of the frame so it again aligns with the inner edge. Mark a line on the frame along the *inner* edge of the lumber, just at the ends; repeat on the opposite side. See the illustration.

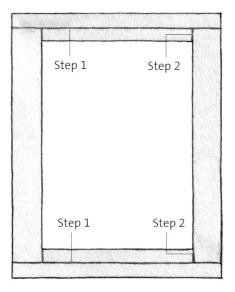

3 Along one side of the frame, measure the distance between the lines marked in Step 1; this is the cut length of the side pieces of lumber. At the top of the frame, measure the distance between the marks made in Step 2; this is the cut length of the top and bottom pieces.

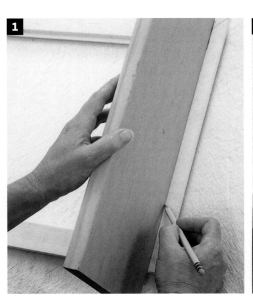

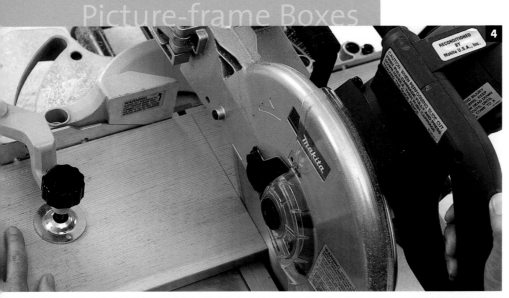

4 Measure and mark the top, bottom, and side pieces on the 1-by-8 lumber. Cut the pieces straight across with the table saw.

5 Prime the frame and 1-by-8 pieces with the latex primer; allow to dry. Paint with two coats of latex paint, allowing the pieces to dry between coats.

6 Using the wood glue and the brad nailer with 1½-inch nails, assemble the box, placing the top and bottom pieces *between* the side pieces.

7 Run a bead of glue around the top edge of the box. Position the frame on the box so the inner edges of the frame and the box are aligned.

8 Brad-nail the frame to the box using the ¾-inch nails, placing three nails in each side piece and two nails each in the top and bottom pieces. Fill the nail holes on the box and the frame with spackling; allow to dry. Sand lightly with the 180-grit sandpaper. Touch up the frame with the latex paint.

Installing the Screwplates

9 Turn the box over so the frame is facedown and the upper edge of the box is toward you. Place a screwplate on one side edge, with the narrower end of the keyhole shape 2½ inches from the upper edge of the box and the wider end of the keyhole shape away from you. Trace the outline of the screwplate; also trace inside the keyhole shape.

10 Using the combination square, make marks at the top and bottom of the keyhole shape. Also make marks at the top and bottom of the screwplate outline. (See the illustration on the next page.)

11 Repeat Steps 9 and 10 on the other side edge.

12 Make a fence to support the router on the center of the box edge (see "Using a Fence"). Position the fence and clamp it to the box.

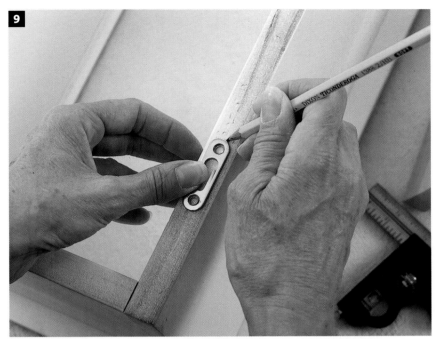

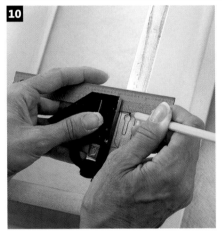

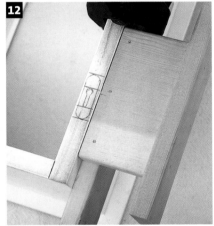

Using a Fence

A fence is a device that guides the router when cutting. For this project, use scrap wood to make a fence similar to the one shown here. The flat surface supports the round soleplate on the router; the raised edge keeps the bit centered on the edge of the box. The exact dimensions of the fence aren't critical, as long as it supports your router and keeps it in the proper position.

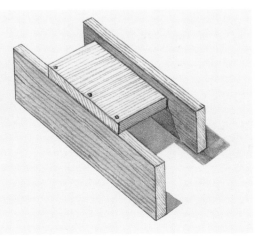

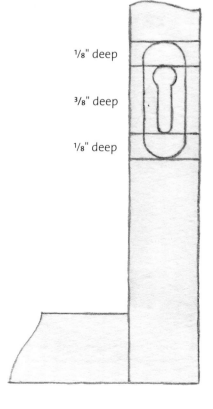

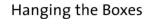

Hanging the Boxes

15 Tape together the sheets of paper to make one large piece several inches wider and longer than the area the boxes will occupy. Lay the paper on the floor and arrange the boxes, measuring and marking the spacing between them carefully to ensure that the boxes are straight in relation to each other. Trace the outline of each box onto the paper as shown below, drawing along the inner and outer edges. Remove the boxes.

16 Turn one box over. Measure from the upper edge of the box to the narrow end of each keyhole shape. On the corresponding box outline, precisely measure and mark the same distances down from the upper edge. Repeat for the other boxes. These marks are for the screws that will go into the wall.

13 Using the router with ½-inch bit, cut a ⅜-inch-deep "trough" from mark to mark *within the key-hole shape only.* Above and below the keyhole shape, cut the screw-plate outline ⅛ inch deep. (See the illustration at left.)

14 Using the screws that came with the screwplates, attach the plates to the box edges, orienting them as shown in the Illustration.

TIP

IT'S FASTEST TO DO ALL THE

ROUTING AT ONCE: MARK

THE SCREWPLATE AND KEY-

HOLE OUTLINES ON ALL BOXES;

CUT THE DEEPER AREAS FIRST,

THEN ADJUST THE DEPTH OF

THE ROUTER AND CUT THE

SHALLOWER AREAS.

⅛" deep

⅜" deep

⅛" deep

17 Pin one corner of the pattern to the wall at the height desired. Have a helper hold up the other end of the pattern. Use the carpenter's level and the upper-edge line on the lowest box to level the pattern; pin the remaining corner of the pattern to the wall.

18 Double-check the measurements taken in Step 16 for each box and the corresponding measurements on each box outline to make sure they match; adjust the marks on the pattern if necessary.

19 Using an awl or a sharp pencil, mark through the pattern and onto the wall at the marks made for the hanging screws. Remove the pattern.

20 Predrill a pilot hole for each nylon anchor; install the anchors.

21 Before you install the hanging screws into the anchors, place one of the screws, head first, into a screwplate and measure the distance showing on the shank. Install each screw into each anchor to that depth.

22 Hang the picture-frame boxes on the screws.

MATERIALS

Square wastebasket

Wallpaper scraps

Scissors

Ruler

Handmade paper,
approximately
22 by 30 inches

Wood scrap (optional)

Waxed paper

Craft brush

All-purpose flat glue*

Rubber stamp

Stamp pad

½-inch-wide ribbon,
equal in length to
the upper edge of the
wastebasket, plus
20 inches

*Does not distort or
warp paper.

DO IT TODAY

Collage Wastebasket

WALLPAPER CUTOUTS, stamped motifs, sheer ribbon, and handmade paper the same shade as the wallpaper background embellish an inexpensive grass-cloth wastebasket. This project works best when the wallpaper shapes are distinct and simple, like the leaves shown here. To find handmade paper, check out craft stores that carry scrapbook and stamping supplies. Many handmade papers have a definite right and wrong side; look closely to determine which side you want to face out.

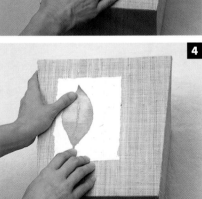

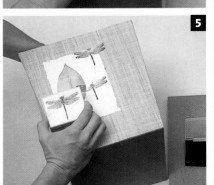

1 Carefully cut out the wallpaper motifs using the scissors. Decide how large to make each handmade paper background piece, allowing a generous area around the motif. Measure and lightly mark each paper piece roughly to size. Crease one marked edge of the paper against the edge of your work surface or against a scrap of wood; carefully tear the paper along the crease. Crease and tear the remaining edges. Make a total of four background pieces.

2 Lay a piece of waxed paper on your work surface. Place a background piece, wrong side up, on the waxed paper. Use the craft brush to apply a thin layer of the glue, brushing beyond the torn edges.

3 Adhere the background piece, off center, to one side of the wastebasket. Smooth the piece with your hand; wipe away any excess glue at the edges with a paper towel.

4 Brush glue onto the wrong side of a wallpaper motif and position it off center on the background piece. Adhere paper and motifs to the remaining sides.

5 Practice stamping on a scrap of the paper. When you determine the quantity of ink and the best pressure to use, stamp the background pieces, overlapping one or more of the edges.

6 Tie the ribbon around the upper edge of the wastebasket; knot the ribbon and position it off center. Tack the ribbon ends to the wastebasket with dots of glue.

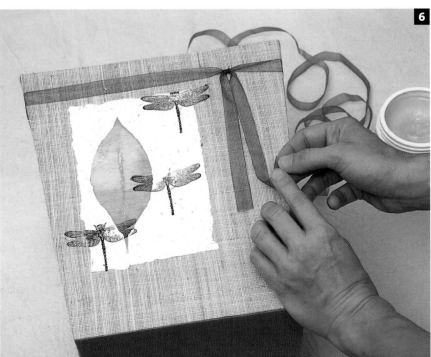

Design Details

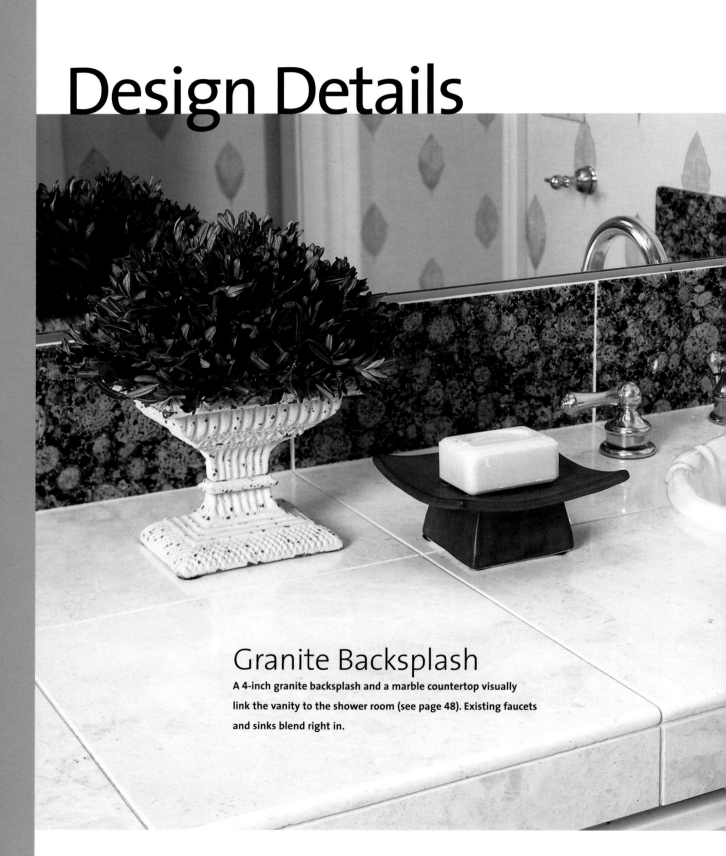

Granite Backsplash

A 4-inch granite backsplash and a marble countertop visually link the vanity to the shower room (see page 48). Existing faucets and sinks blend right in.

Robe Hook

LEFT: **When space is at a premium, robe hooks are a practical alternative to towel bars. Not a part of an ensemble, this brushed-nickel-and-brass hook just happens to echo the forms and finishes of the light bar.**

Light Bar

BELOW: **A brushed-nickel light bar, accented in brass, works well with both existing and new fixtures.**

Shower Niche

RIGHT: A recessed shelf offers a spot to stow shower gear and adds an architectural element to the space.

Fixture Update

LEFT: Metals mix easily in this brushed-nickel-and-brass shower fixture (see Resources, page 142), chosen to harmonize with the nickel hardware on the shower door and the brass handle on the toilet.

Shower Makeover

RIGHT: Awkward steps took up valuable space in the small tub-shower area. Accentuating the closed-in feeling were a fixed-glass window covered with blinds and a conventional curtain on a rod.
LEFT: Removing the steps and the tub and tiling the walls with 12-inch white marble tiles and 6-inch granite squares created an elegant walk-in shower with a glass door. A new transom window with obscuring glass provides natural ventilation and ensures privacy.

Nantucket Charm

EVERYTHING'S POSITIVELY SHIPSHAPE now, thanks to a lighter and brighter palette and an array of new components. Beadboard paneling with cap and base molding gives the room much-needed "bones." A pedestal sink in place of the original vanity opens up the space and directs attention to the diagonal tile floor. A narrow window with wide wood casing appears larger with the addition of a traditional louvered shutter. Paint and fabric turn an unfinished bookcase with beadboard detailing into a curtained cupboard. Shiny chrome fixtures complete the nautical look.

BEFORE: Drab wallpaper, large wood furniture pieces, and a dull vinyl floor made this diminutive bath seem even smaller.

4- by 8-foot
beadboard panels*
(see Resources, page 142)

¾- by 2-inch cap molding*

3½-inch base molding*

¾-inch corner guard trim

¼-inch quarter-
round molding
(optional; see Step 24)

Carpenter's level

Circular saw

Paneling and molding
adhesive

Caulking gun

Wood block

Brad nailer with ⅝ -, 1-,
and 1½-inch nails

4-foot metal
straightedge (optional)

Clamps (optional)

Latex primer (see Step 17)

2½-inch paintbrush

Stud finder

Miter box with backsaw

Spackling

Painter's caulk

220-grit sandpaper

Blue painter's tape

Latex paint

*See Step 1 for quantity.

MAKEOVER MAGIC

Beadboard

PANELS MADE OF ¼-inch-thick MDF (medium-density fiberboard) are an inexpensive alternative to traditional tongue-and-groove beadboard. Installation is relatively simple, but for professional-looking results you'll need to know how to *scribe* a vertical edge on the panels and *cope* one half of a mitered joint on the molding. Consult a carpentry book for instructions and tools. Beadboard paneling can be installed only on flat walls; check with a carpenter's level to make sure yours aren't bowed.

FINISHED SIZE 48 inches high

Getting Started

1 These panels are 48 inches high, making it possible to cut two pieces from one 4- by 8-foot panel. Make a bird's-eye sketch of the room, with dimensions, to determine how many full panels and how many feet of cap and base molding you will need. Have the panels cut for you. Add 10 percent to the molding footage for cutting errors.

2 Remove existing baseboards.

3 Condition the beadboard panels and the molding by bringing them indoors, preferably into the room where they will be installed, 3 to 5 days before you begin.

4 If you are keeping existing flooring, or if new flooring is already installed, skip to the next step. If you will be installing flooring later, make ¼-inch spacers to raise the panels off the underlayment.

Installing the Panels

5 Start the beadboard at an inside corner. Place the first panel against the wall, orienting it according to the arrows on the back. With a carpenter's level, check for plumb along one vertical edge. To achieve plumb, you may need to trim the lower edge with the circular saw. You may also need to scribe the vertical edge that goes into the corner.

6 With the panel in position, lightly draw a line on the wall along the upper edge of the panel.

7 Turn the panel over so the wrong side is facing you. Using the paneling and molding adhesive in the caulking gun, apply a ¼-inch bead of adhesive in wavy lines. Do not apply adhesive within ½ inch of the edges.

TIP

EACH PANEL HAS A BEAD ON ONE EDGE AND NO BEAD ON THE OTHER EDGE, RESULTING IN A SEAMLESS LOOK ONCE THE PANELS ARE INSTALLED. ARROWS ON THE BACK ENSURE THAT YOU ORIENT THEM CORRECTLY. WHEN YOU BUY THE PANELS, ASK IF THE MANUFAC-TURER MAKES CAP MOLDING TO MATCH.

8 Turn the panel over again and set it in place, aligning the upper edge with the marked line on the wall. Put the block behind the lower edge of the panel to hold it 6 to 8 inches from the wall for several minutes, until the adhesive becomes tacky. Remove the block and push the lower edge into place, making sure the upper edge is still at the marked line. Press the panel against the wall firmly and evenly.

9 Using the brad nailer and the ⅝-inch nails, shoot the nails at a downward angle through the beadboard and into the wall, spacing them approximately 10 inches apart on the upper, lower, and side edges.

10 Install the adjoining panels in the same manner, spacing them ⅟₁₆ inch apart or according to the manufacturer's instructions. As you add panels, you may need to trim the lower edges with the circular saw to maintain plumb.

11 When you reach the next corner, measure, mark, and cut the panel as needed to fit. (A 4-foot metal straightedge clamped to the panel makes a stable guide when a lengthwise cut is needed.)

Turning an Inside Corner

12 Return to the corner where you began. Butt the edge of a new panel against the first panel. Scribe the edge of the new panel if necessary; glue and nail the panel. Install the remaining panels on that wall, cutting the end panel to fit.

13 When you turn the next inside corner, cut the new panel so the beadboard design flows uninterrupted. For example, if the just-attached panel was cut in the middle of a bead, the next panel should be cut in the same spot, to make it look as if the panel continues around the corner.

Turning an Outside Corner

14 In this bathroom, a partial wall near the tub creates two closely placed outside corners. To turn the first outside corner, measure, mark, and cut the panel ¼ inch (or the thickness of the beadboard) beyond the edge of the first outside corner, as shown in the bird's-eye illustration below. Glue and nail the piece.

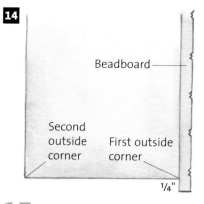

15 Measure, mark, and cut the next piece of beadboard so it fits against the previous piece and extends ¼ inch beyond the second outside corner, as shown above right. Glue and nail the piece.

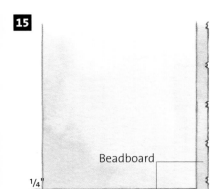

15

Beadboard

1/4"

16 Glue and nail the next piece of beadboard, fitting it against the previous piece and continuing along the wall. Attach additional panels to complete the room.

TIP

FOR A PEDESTAL SINK, CUT
HOLES FOR THE WATER AND
DRAIN LINES USING A DRILL
WITH A HOLE SAW ATTACH-
MENT AND A JIGSAW.

Attaching the Moldings

17 If you're not working with already-primed materials, prime the molding. Install the molding in this order: cap, base, and corner guard.

18 Using the stud finder, locate the studs and lightly mark their location on the wall, just above the upper edge of the panels. Measure, mark, and cut the cap molding, using the miter box with backsaw. (If desired, cope one piece on each inside corner.)

19 With the brad nailer and the 1½-inch nails, attach the cap molding at the thickest part, nailing through the beadboard and into the studs.

20 Remove the spacers and install the flooring now, before attaching the base molding.

21 Mark the studs on the bead-board near the floor.

22 Measure, mark, and cut the base molding. (If desired, cope one

piece on each inside corner.) Attach the molding to the beadboard using the 1½-inch nails, nailing into the studs.

23 Measure, mark, and cut the corner guard molding. Attach the molding to the outside corners using the 1-inch nails.

24 In less-than-perfect inside corners, install quarter-round molding.

Finishing the Beadboard

25 Fill the nail holes with spack-ling. Use painter's caulk to fill any gaps between the molding and the wall. Allow to dry. Sand with the 220-grit sandpaper.

26 With the painter's tape, mask off the wall above the cap molding and the floor below the base mold-ing. Using the latex paint and the 2½-inch brush, paint the beadboard and the molding. Allow the paint to dry. Sand the beadboard and the molding lightly and apply a second coat of paint.

19

21

23

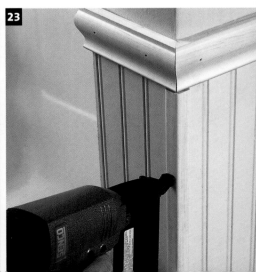

MATERIALS

Steel tape measure

24-inch carpenter's square

3-foot metal straightedge

VCT in two colors to total the room's square footage, plus 15 percent[*] (see Resources, page 142)

Rubber or latex gloves

Knee pads

Vinyl tile adhesive

Vinyl tile adhesive trowel

Clean cloths

Rolling pin

Utility knife

Rotary cutting mat, 22 by 34 inches or larger, available at fabric stores and quilt shops

Blue painter's tape

Mineral spirits

Buffable acrylic floor finish

Be sure to buy "vinyl composition tile," not the peel-and-stick variety.

IN A WEEKEND

Vinyl Tile Floor

A BLUE-AND-WHITE CHECKERBOARD PATTERN creates the illusion of more space in this small bath and provides a pleasing contrast to the straight-up-and-down lines of the beadboard wall panels. Commercial-grade vinyl composition tile, known as VCT, is 12 inches square and comes in boxes of 45 pieces of the same color. Be sure to use a trowel designed just for VCT adhesive; other trowels apply too much adhesive, preventing it from setting up properly.

TIP

WHEN PLANNING THE LAYOUT FOR DIAGONAL TILE, START WITH AN INTERIOR TILE AND WORK OUTWARD. IN THIS ROOM, THE FIRST TILE WAS CENTERED ON THE DOORWAY AND DOWN THE GALLEY PORTION OF THE ROOM. SEE THE ILLUSTRATION AT RIGHT.

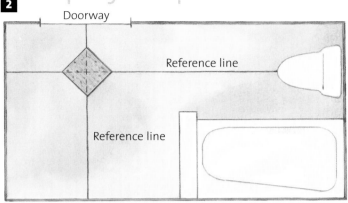

Doorway

Reference line

Reference line

Preparing the Surface

1 If your underlayment is not perfectly smooth—which it will not be if you rip out existing sheet vinyl—you'll need to replace it (see page 131) or have it replaced by a flooring installer.

2 Using the steel tape, carpenter's square, and long metal straightedge, carefully measure and draw reference lines on the underlayment that intersect at a 90-degree angle, indicating the center of the first tile.

3 Choose the darker tile for your first piece. Lay it over the center so its corners align precisely with the reference lines.

4 Hold the tile firmly in place—better yet, have a helper stand on it. Using the metal straightedge, draw guidelines along two adjoining edges of the tile; extend the lines 24 inches in both directions. These will be your initial placement lines for the diagonal pattern. Make the lines dark so you can see them through the adhesive once it's applied.

Setting Tiles

5 Put the tile aside. Wearing the gloves and the knee pads, spread adhesive thinly and evenly with the trowel, covering the area marked by the placement lines. Allow the adhesive to set up according to the manufacturer's instructions.

6 Lower the first tile into place, lining up its edges precisely with the placement lines. Press firmly.

7 Lay a lighter-colored tile, lining it up precisely with the first tile and the placement lines.

8 Lay a darker tile, followed by a lighter tile, to complete a unit of four tiles (see the tip at right).

9 Continue spreading adhesive and laying full tiles until you reach the point where you must cut tiles to fit. Clean excess adhesive off the tiles with a clean cloth and warm, soapy water. (If the adhesive has dried, see Step 18.)

10 Go over the laid tiles with the rolling pin to set them.

Cutting Tiles to Fit

11 To cut tiles to fit around a heating/cooling register and the waste hole, first warm the tiles using a hair dryer. Cut carefully with the utility knife.

12 You'll need to cut partial tiles to fill in the floor area near the walls. Measure the area to be covered by a partial tile as shown in the illustration at left. Make sure you hold the tape straight when you measure.

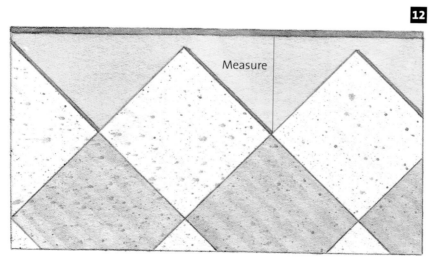

Measure

13 Line up the tile to be cut with the 45-degree-angle lines on the rotary cutting mat, as shown at top right. Tape two adjoining edges to the mat using the blue painter's tape. Lay the steel tape over the tile, aligning the measurement you took in Step 12 with the point of the tile. Lay the metal straightedge perpendicular to the end of the tape, using the cutting lines on the mat as a guide. Mark the tile along the straightedge.

14 Using the metal straightedge and the utility knife, firmly score the tile along the marked line.

15 Snap the tile. Smooth the snapped edge against a scrap tile. The snapped edges on partial tiles need not be perfect—they will be covered by the baseboards.

16 Spread adhesive on the area, being careful not to get it on the already-set tiles. Allow the adhesive to set up; lay the cut tile.

17 Continue cutting and setting partial tiles to complete the floor. Go over the tiles with the rolling pin.

Finishing the Floor

18 Clean up dried adhesive on the tile with mineral spirits and a clean cloth. Lightly wash the surface with mild soap and water to remove the residue. Allow the tile and the adhesive to "cure" overnight.

19 Apply the acrylic floor finish according to the manufacturer's instructions.

20 Reattach the baseboards.

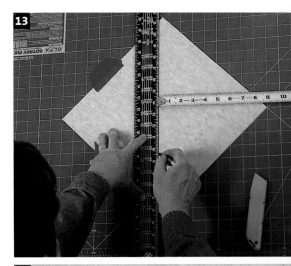

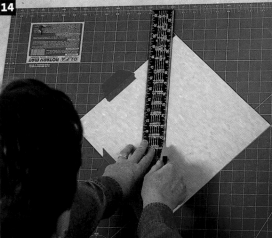

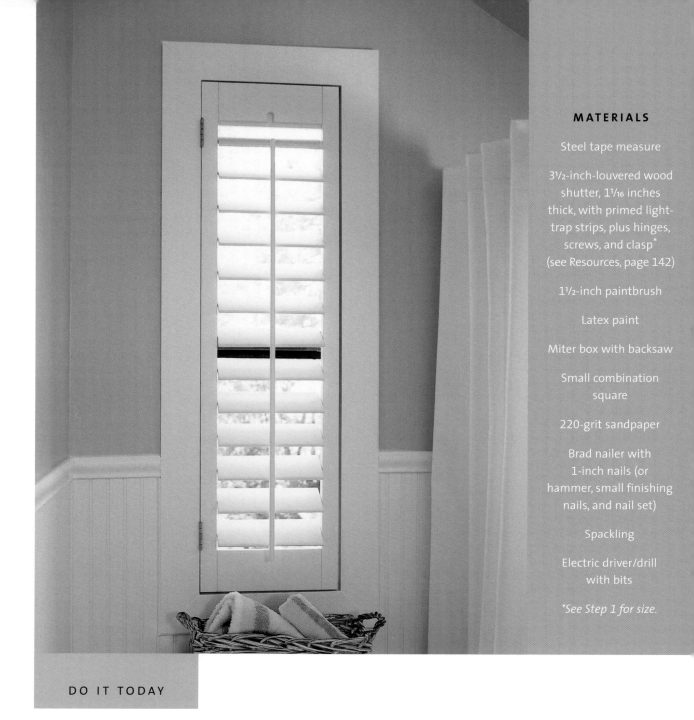

MATERIALS

Steel tape measure

3½-inch-louvered wood shutter, 1¹⁄₁₆ inches thick, with primed light-trap strips, plus hinges, screws, and clasp* (see Resources, page 142)

1½-inch paintbrush

Latex paint

Miter box with backsaw

Small combination square

220-grit sandpaper

Brad nailer with 1-inch nails (or hammer, small finishing nails, and nail set)

Spackling

Electric driver/drill with bits

*See Step 1 for size.

DO IT TODAY

Shutter

THIS SHUTTER WAS INSTALLED in a window whose jamb meets the casing at right angles, with no traditional windowsill. For a window with a rounded casing and a protruding sill, you'll need to determine how far into the opening to inset the shutter; discuss the placement with the shutter supplier. Keep in mind that the farther in you place the shutter, the narrower its open-and-close range of motion.

FINISHED SIZE

13 by 46½ inches

Measuring the Window

1 Measure the length and width of your window opening in three places—at the midpoint and at each end. If the measurements in either direction vary more than 1/16 inch, consult a window treatment installer; a shutter may not be appropriate for your window. If the measurements vary 1/16 inch or less, use the minimum measurement in each direction when ordering the shutter.

Installing the Light-trap Strips

2 Using the 1½-inch brush, paint the light-trap strips with the latex paint. Allow the paint to dry.

3 Set a light-trap strip on the windowsill, with one of its ¾-inch edges resting on the sill. Mark the strip to equal the width of the window opening.

4 Cut the strip straight across using the miter box with backsaw.

5 Using the small combination square, mark the sill 1⅛ inches (or the required distance into the opening) from the front edge, near the center; repeat at both ends.

6 Insert the light-trap strip into the windowsill—it will be snug— with the ¾-inch side facing down, lining up the front edge of the strip *just behind* the marks made in the previous step. If necessary, lightly sand one end of the strip with the 220-grit sandpaper to make it fit. Nail the strip to the sill at the ends and every 6 inches.

7 Repeat Steps 3 through 6 to attach the upper light-trap strip.

8 Measure, mark, and cut the side light-trap strips to fit snugly between the upper and lower strips. Install each side strip.

9 If you're using finishing nails, countersink them with the nail set. Fill the nail holes with spackling; allow to dry. Sand. Touch up the strips with paint.

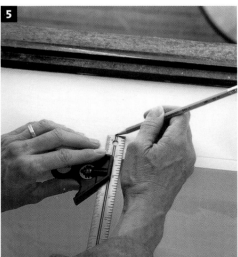

12 Remove the shutter. Pull out the hinge pins and remove the unattached flanges. With the aid of a helper, position a flange in the window jamb so it aligns with the marks you made in the previous step. Align the edge of the flange flush with the front edge of the window opening as shown; screw the flange into the window jamb. Repeat to attach the other flange. Set the shutter in place and reinsert the pins.

Attaching the Clasp

13 The clasp consists of a rounded "button" that fits into a "receiver." First install the receiver on the sill light-trap strip, using the screws provided. Insert the button into the receiver. Close the shutter and press it against the button; the small screw in the button will mark the frame of the shutter. Open shutter and remove the button from the receiver. Screw the button into the frame at the mark. Adjust the clasp tension with pliers if necessary.

TIP

NEVER OPEN THE SHUTTER BY PULLING ON THE TILT BAR. INSTEAD, TILT THE LOUVERS, REACH IN, AND OPEN THE SHUTTER BY ITS FRAME.

Attaching the Hinges

10 Using the electric driver/drill and screws, attach each hinge to the shutter, with the edge of the flange flush with the back edge of the shutter as shown. Be sure the hinges are oriented in the correct direction. (They usually have arrows or "top" marked on them.)

11 Set the shutter into the window jamb. Use coins to shim up the shutter at the bottom to create equal space at the top and bottom of the window opening. Carefully mark the jamb at the top and the bottom of each hinge.

Beadboard bookcase
with three shelves
(see Resources, page 142)

Six wood knobs

2½-inch paintbrush

Latex primer

180-grit sandpaper

Yellow and white latex
paint, satin finish
(see Resources, page 142)

Latex glazing medium

Soft cotton cloths

Electric driver/drill
with a drill bit the same
diameter as the
knob shank

Wood glue

Steel tape measure

White cotton duck,
54 inches wide*

Fabric scissors

White thread

6- by 24-inch acrylic
rotary ruler, available at
fabric stores and
quilt shops

Pale-colored fabric
marker

Pins

*See Step 9 for yardage;
add ¼ yard for ties.

IN A WEEKEND

Cottage Cupboard

PAINT AND LATEX GLAZING MEDIUM transform an unfinished bookcase
with beadboard sides and back into a freestanding storage cupboard.
Cotton-duck curtain panels tied to wooden knobs couldn't be easier to
sew. To preserve the fabric's crisp finish, dry-clean rather than wash the
panels. Bookcases usually come with removable shelves and shelf "pins"
that allow you to set the shelves at any position.

FINISHED SIZE 48 inches wide, 12 inches deep, 60 inches tall

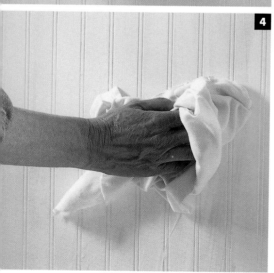

Painting the Bookcase

1 Prime the bookcase, shelves, and wood knobs, using the 2½-inch paintbrush and the latex primer; allow to dry according to the manufacturer's instructions. Sand with the 180-grit sandpaper.

2 Paint the bookcase, shelves, and knobs with the yellow latex paint; allow to dry. Sand. Apply a second coat of paint.

3 Mix equal parts of white latex paint and glazing medium. Brush the mixture onto the bookcase, covering a 2- by 2-foot area. Proceed to the next step immediately.

4 Using a cotton cloth, wipe most of the paint-glazing mixture off the surface, leaving more of the mixture in the grooves of the beadboard.

5 Repeat Steps 3 and 4 on the rest of the bookcase, the shelves, and the knobs. Allow the paint to dry.

Attaching the Knobs

6 Insert the middle shelf into the bookcase. Measure and mark the knob placement. Each outer knob on this bookcase is 2 inches from the side; each inner knob is 1 inch from the midpoint of the shelf, creating a 2-inch space at the center. The other knobs are centered between the outer and inner knobs.

7 Using the electric driver/drill, drill holes for the knobs at the marks.

8 Apply wood glue to the shank of each knob. Insert the knobs into the holes. Wipe away excess glue.

Making the Panels

9 Measure the width and length of the opening below the middle shelf. (Make sure you measure just the *opening,* not the distances from outside edge to outside edge.) Divide the width measurement by 2; add 2¼ inches to arrive at the cut width *of each panel.* Add 2¼ inches to the length measurement to arrive at the cut length *of each panel.* Carefully cut two curtain panels on the lengthwise grain of the fabric.

10 Zigzag the raw edges of each panel to prevent them from raveling.

11 On the right side of each panel, lightly mark hemlines 1 inch from the top, bottom, and side edges, using the rotary ruler and the fabric marker. (The lines will intersect near the corners.) From each corner, mark a point 2 inches along each edge, as shown; connect the marks to create a diagonal line.

12 Turn one panel wrong side up. Turn up the fabric along the diagonal line at a corner and press. Press the remaining corners in the same way. Repeat on the other panel.

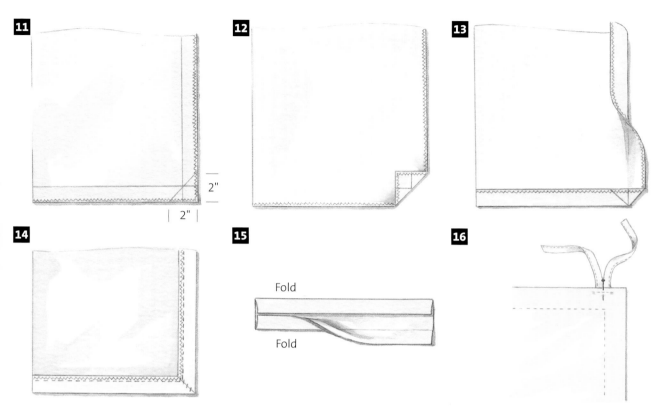

11 2" | 2" |

12

13

14

15 Fold Fold

16

13 Press the hems of both panels to the wrong side along the marked lines. Pin.

14 Using a straight stitch, sew the hems by machine close to the zigzagged edges, pivoting at the corners. Slipstitch the miters closed.

15 From the remaining duck fabric, measure, mark, and cut 12 pieces, each 1½ by 5 inches, to make ties for the knobs. Fold a piece in half lengthwise, wrong sides together, and press; open the strip and fold in the raw edges to meet the pressed fold. Refold the strip and re-press. Pin; machine-stitch close to the folded edges. Using a short zigzag stitch, finish one raw end. Repeat to make the remaining ties.

16 On the right side of each panel at the upper edge, insert a pin to mark the location of each knob. On either side of each pin, place the unstitched end of a tie on the wrong side of the panel; orient the stitched edges of the ties as shown. Pin and stitch the ties to the panels from the right side, stitching through all thicknesses and backstitching at the start and finish to secure the threads.

17 Loosely tie the curtain panels to the knobs.

17

Clean &
Crisp

Chrome Fixtures

**An oval tilt mirror, a pair of sconces, and a glass shelf provide sparkle
and neutral "color" in the blue, white, and yellow scheme.**

Widespread Faucet

ABOVE: **With its graceful lever handles, this old-fashioned faucet completes the pedestal sink in vintage style (see Resources, page 142).**

Bucket Wastebasket

RIGHT: **A French floral bucket, painted white to match the beadboard, makes an out-of-the-ordinary wastebasket.**

Robe Hooks

LEFT: **Matching hooks gleam against a backdrop of white beadboard and help keep everything in its place.**

Artwork

LEFT: **This harbor scene served as the color catalyst for the room's scheme. A distressed-wood frame makes a subtle contrast to smooth, sky blue walls.**

Step Stool

BELOW: **An unfinished wood stool painted the same yellow as the storage cupboard repeats a key color, with a bit more emphasis.**

Shower Curtain

**A grommeted cotton curtain hanging on a wire "rod"
covers up a standard sliding tub-shower door.**

Natural Bent

AN ABUNDANCE OF EARTHY COLORS and materials sets the tone for this garden-style room. A potting bench–turned-vanity establishes the theme. Lime paint in a shade called "putty" lends subtle visual texture to walls stenciled in plant motifs. Underfoot, natural slate tiles form a random pattern in an array of organic hues. A ceiling-mounted cornice and floor-length shower curtain cover existing tile and add a touch of sophistication (see page 85). Reflective surfaces—an oval mirror and a glass tile "curtain"—bounce light around the room, enhancing the outdoor connection.

BEFORE: Unremarkable in every way, a small master bath with stock cabinetry and tile begged for a bold approach and an imaginative scheme.

MATERIALS

Stencil plastic for each motif pattern

Permanent marker

Rotary cutting mat, available at fabric stores and quilt shops

Craft knife

Repositionable spray adhesive

Pushpins

4-inch joint knife

All-purpose, ready-mixed joint compound, available at home centers and paint stores (see the tip on the facing page)

Sanding block, medium-fine grit

Undercoat sealer*

Paint tray with disposable liners

Paint roller with ¼-inch roller cover

2½-inch paintbrush

Lime paint*

6-inch box brush

Matte-finish wall sealer*

*Use the sealers recommended by the lime paint manufacturer. See Resources, page 142.

MAKEOVER MAGIC

Lime Paint Walls

PAINT THAT CONTAINS LIME behaves differently from other paints. When wet, it appears dark and dull; as it dries, it "blooms," creating a lighter, slightly mottled effect. The color continues to evolve until the walls are sealed. Lime paint requires patience and extra effort to apply, but the result is a one-of-a-kind, natural wall treatment. Here, lime paint was combined with bas-relief motifs for an even richer effect.

Making the Patterns

1 Enlarge the patterns on pages 73 through 75 to the indicated dimensions.

2 Determine the placement of the motifs and lightly mark the walls. Strive for varied angles and random distribution of shapes, keeping them away from baseboards, shower curtain rods, and other items that are flush with the wall.

Making the Stencils

The following instructions are for creating a raised rectangular area and a recessed leaf motif within it. For a raised motif only, such as the leaf on page 69, make a stencil with just the motif cut out.

3 Lay stencil plastic over the enlarged pattern, allowing several inches of plastic beyond the pattern's rectangular outline. Trace the leaf and the rectangle with the permanent marker.

4 Working on the rotary cutting mat, cut on the lines using the craft knife. Keep the leaf shape and the outer "frame" piece. (You can see these two pieces in photo 6.) Set aside the piece in between.

Applying the Compound

5 Cover your work surface with paper towels. Spray the back of each part of the stencil with repositionable adhesive.

6 Position the leaf and the outer piece on the wall and press firmly to adhere. Insert a pushpin at one end of the leaf to allow you to pull it away once it's covered with joint compound.

7 Using the joint knife, apply the compound to the wall, over the stencil plastic and through the open area. Spread the compound 1/16 to 1/8 inch thick, striving for a slightly irregular surface, as if frosting a cake. Go over the area several times to release any air bubbles.

8 Carefully lift the "frame" piece. Gently pull out the pushpin and lift the leaf, revealing the recessed motif.

TIP THE MOTIFS WILL SEEM INTEGRAL TO THE WALLS IF THE WALLS ARE FIRST COVERED WITH THE SAME JOINT COMPOUND USED TO CREATE THE RELIEF DESIGNS, THEN SMOOTHED WITH A METAL DRYWALL-TAPING KNIFE.

6
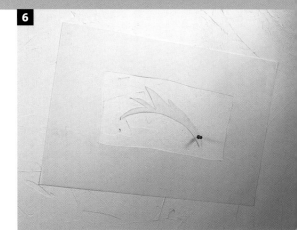

7

8a

8b

11

13

9 Wash the compound off the stencil pieces and wipe them dry.

10 Stencil the remaining motifs in the same way. Allow the compound to dry overnight, until it is light and uniform in color.

11 Using the sanding block, lightly sand the edges of each motif and any other areas that are noticeably rough.

Painting the Walls

12 Apply the undercoat sealer with the paint roller according to the manufacturer's instructions. Work the sealer into the recessed areas with the 2½-inch paintbrush. Allow to dry.

13 Apply the lime paint with the 6-inch box brush in a broad, cross-hatching motion. Be sure to work the paint into the recessed areas. Allow to dry 6 hours. Apply a second and third coat, allowing at least 6 hours between coats.

14 Using the paint roller or box brush, apply the matte sealer. (Avoid overloading the roller or the brush with sealer—it tends to run.) Use the 2½-inch brush to work the sealer into the recessed areas. Don't be alarmed at the color of the sealer; it goes on milky (and darkens the paint), but it all dries to the proper color.

TIP

TO MAINTAIN A WET EDGE AND PREVENT STOP-AND-START LINES, HAVE A HELPER APPLY THE LIME PAINT AT THE CEILING LINE AND IN THE CORNERS WITH THE 2½-INCH BRUSH WHILE YOU COVER THE LARGE AREAS WITH THE BOX BRUSH.

14

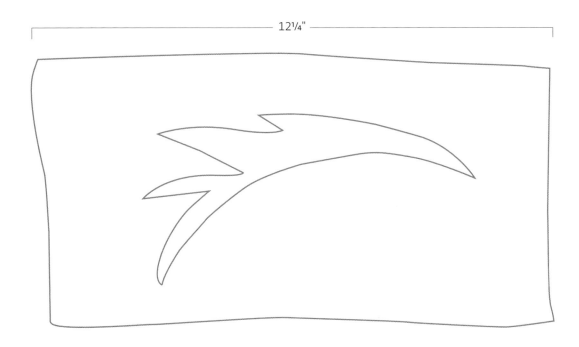

12¼"

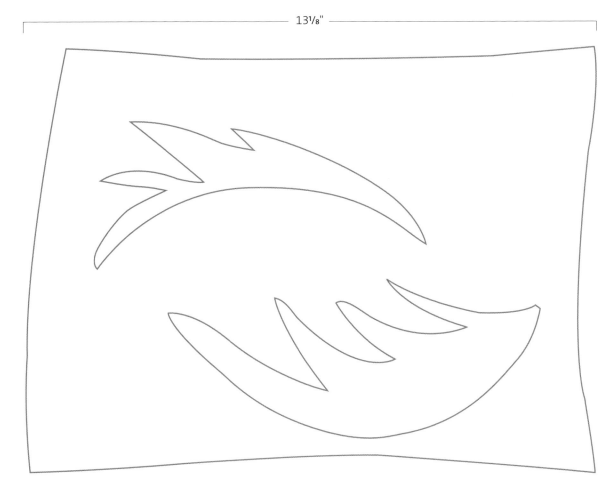

13⅛"

Stencil patterns. See Step 1 on page 71. (The rectangles above can also be combined with the larger motifs on the following page; see the photo on page 70.)

11³/₈"

11³/₈

Stencil patterns. See Step 1 on page 71.

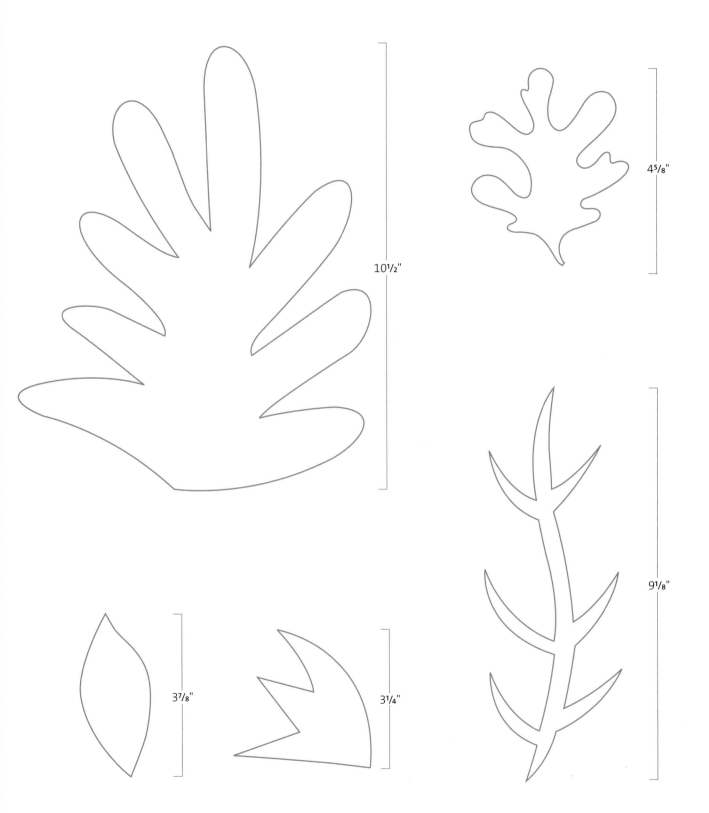

10½"

4⁵⁄₈"

9¹⁄₈"

3⁷⁄₈"

3¹⁄₄"

Slate Floor

INSTALLING SLATE TILE is relatively simple, thanks to the natural qualities of the stone and a new underlayment material. Slate is soft, making it easy to cut and nip. These tiles are "gauged," meaning each piece was milled to the same thickness. The polyethylene-membrane underlayment used in this project is much easier to install than traditional cement board and creates a smooth, waterproof surface on which to set the slate. It also absorbs and releases pressure, minimizing the possibility of tiles cracking.

MATERIALS

Gauged slate tiles,
13 inches square
(see Resources, page 142)

Polyethylene-membrane
underlayment

Steel tape measure

Utility knife and metal
straightedge, or heavy-
duty scissors

Electric driver/drill with
mortar mixing bit and
hole saw attachment

Thinset adhesive

5-gallon bucket

³/₁₆- by ¼-inch
V-notched trowel

Paint stir sticks

Pull saw

China marker or
wax pencil

Eye and ear protection

Heavy-duty rubber or
latex gloves

Wet saw

Tile nippers

³/₈- by ¼-inch
square-notched trowel

Wedge spacers,
super size

Penetrating sealer for
tile, marble, and grout

Cotton cloths

Acrylic mortar and
grout additive

Sanded grout

Grout float

Tile sponge

2-inch blue painter's
tape

Caulking grout to match
sanded grout

Stone color enhancer,
matte finish

3-inch paintbrush

Planning the Layout

1 Remove the baseboards and the existing flooring down to the subfloor. (If you're planning to paint the walls, do so now.) Remove the toilet and set it aside.

2 Take the tiles outdoors and arrange them as desired, starting at what will be the most conspicuous corner. (It's helpful to start your layout in a corner near the toilet; that way, you'll be able to cut the tiles around the waste-line hole more accurately.) Leave gaps of roughly ¼ inch between tiles, and place full tiles for those that will be cut to fit at the edges. Hose off the slate thoroughly; allow to dry.

Installing the Underlayment

3 The underlayment goes on the floor mesh side down. Measure and mark the underlayment to fit the room; cut using the utility knife and metal straightedge or the scissors. Cut out the hole for the waste line. Do a dry-run placement of the underlayment to check the fit; trim as needed and set aside.

4 Using the electric driver/drill and the mortar mixing bit, prepare the thinset adhesive to the consistency of thin batter.

5 Holding the straight edge of the V-notched trowel at a 45-degree angle, spread the thinset over the subfloor. Holding the notched edge of the trowel at a 45- to 90-degree angle, comb the thinset, creating ridges.

6 Roll the underlayment onto the thinset, mesh side down.

7 Using the straight edge of the V-notched trowel, apply even, downward pressure to "smoosh" the underlayment into the thinset. As the thinset fills the indentations, the underlayment will darken slightly.

5

6

7

Cutting Contours and Holes

8 Do a dry-run placement of the tiles, spacing them roughly ¼ inch apart, starting in the designated corner and working to the toilet. (Slate tiles are not always perfectly square, allowing you to eyeball the spacing between pieces rather than using standard tile spacers.)

9 Mark tile as needed to follow contours at the floor's edges, such as around the tub.

10 It's easier to trim a doorjamb and slide the slate under it than to make a complex cut in the tile. To trim the jamb, lay a scrap tile on the underlayment, with paint stir sticks under the slate to allow for the depth of the thinset. With the pull saw flat on the tile, trim the jamb.

11 To accommodate the waste hole, position one of the tiles that will partially fit around the hole. Find a plate the same size as the hole or make a template.

12 Align the plate or the template with the hole and mark the curve on the tile using the china marker or the wax pencil.

13 Place the adjoining tile to cover the hole. Align the plate or the template with the curve marked on the first tile. Mark the adjoining tile to complete the circle.

14 Put on the eye and ear protection and the gloves. Using the wet saw, make straight cuts toward the curve marked on each tile, leaving ¼-inch slivers of slate between the cuts.

15 Using the tile nippers, break off the slivers.

16 Nip away at the edges, all the way to the marked curve.

17 Cut gentle contours, like the one shown in Step 9, with a combination of plain cuts for straight lines and nipped cuts for curves.

18 Using the hole saw attachment on the driver/drill, cut holes in the appropriate tile or tiles for the heating/cooling register (see page 91). Or simply cut the tile to accommodate the register.

Spreading Thinset on the Underlayment

19 Mix a second batch of thinset to the consistency of thick frosting. Let it sit 5 to 10 minutes; remix. (You can add powder to any leftover thinset from Step 4 to stiffen it.) Holding the straight edge of the square-notched trowel at a 45-degree angle, spread the thinset over the underlayment for the first row of tiles, filling the indentations. It's easier to pull the thinset toward you than to push it away.

20 Holding the notched edge of the square-notched trowel at a 45- to 90-degree angle, comb the thinset, creating ridges. The ridges should hold their shape; if they don't, scrape off the thinset, add powder, remix, and spread it again.

Setting the Tile

21 Set the first tile in the corner determined in Step 2. Continue setting full tiles in rows, spacing them evenly and gently "smooshing" the pieces into the thinset. Wipe thinset off the surface as you go.

TIP

DO NOT STAND OR CRAWL ON JUST-SET SLATE FOR AT LEAST 24 HOURS. DEPENDING ON THE CONFIGURATION OF YOUR BATHROOM, YOU MAY NEED TO STOP WORK UNTIL THE NEXT DAY, WHEN YOU CAN WALK ON PREVIOUSLY LAID AREAS.

22 Continue setting full pieces until you reach the point where you must cut tiles at the edges.

23 Measure, mark, and cut partial tiles to complete the floor. If your floor is square and the pieces will be the same size, you can set the fence on the wet saw and cut all the pieces at one time.

24 Set the partial tiles. For pieces that go under the doorjamb, spread thinset on the appropriate edges and slide the pieces in place.

Setting the Baseboard

25 Measure and mark tiles 4 inches wide for the baseboard pieces. Cut the pieces on the wet saw.

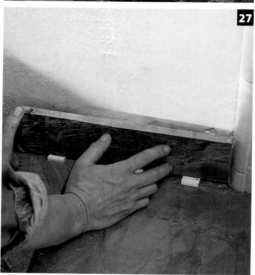

26 Place wedge spacers, with their narrow edges to the wall, on the floor tile in the starting corner. "Back-butter" a base piece as shown.

27 Rest the base piece on the spacers and press it firmly against the wall.

28 Add adjoining base pieces, eyeballing the spacing and placing spacers underneath. Cut pieces to fit when you reach the corners.

Applying the Penetrating Sealer

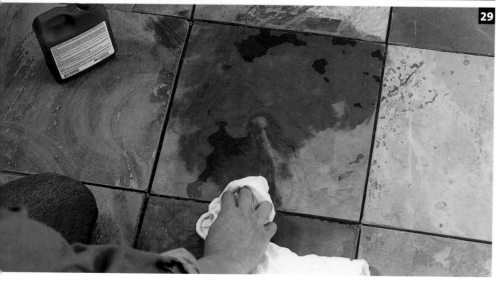

29 Because slate is porous, you must apply a penetrating sealer to prevent the grout from staining the tiles. Use a cotton cloth and follow the manufacturer's instructions.

Allow a little of the sealer to run over the edges of the tiles to keep the grout from "bleeding" at the edges. Allow the sealer to dry.

Grouting the Joints

30 Acrylic additive makes the grout stronger and helps it retain its color. Mix the additive with water according to the manufacturer's instructions.

31 Mix the liquid from the previous step and the grout powder according to the manufacturer's instructions. Using the grout float held at a 45-degree angle, push the grout into the joints, working diagonally and packing the grout as firmly as possible. Also apply the grout between the base pieces and where the base pieces meet the floor. Do not apply grout across the top of the base pieces.

32 As soon as a haze forms, use a wrung-out tile sponge to clean the grout from the surface. Wipe only the surface of the slate, not the grouted joints, to prevent washing out the grout. Clean the surface again and again, rinsing the sponge often, until the haze disappears. Allow to dry.

33 Mask the wall with the blue painter's tape just above the top of the base pieces. Run a bead of caulking grout along the upper edge of the base pieces; use a gloved finger to push the caulking grout into the small gaps between the pieces and the wall. Wipe off the excess with a damp cloth.

34 When the caulking grout is dry, carefully pull off the tape at a 45-degree angle.

35 Allow the grout to cure 3 days. Apply the stone color enhancer with the 3-inch brush.

MATERIALS

Electric driver/drill

Potting bench

Bar sink* and farm-style
faucet (see Resources,
page 142)

Waterproof marker

Hole saw attachment
recommended by the
faucet manufacturer

½-inch drill bit

Jigsaw

Steel tape measure

Circular saw or miter
box with backsaw

1-by-2 lumber for braces
(see Step 6)

½-inch brad-point drill bit

Eight #6 wood screws,
1½ inches long

Wood glue

Eight wood plugs,
½ inch in diameter and
¼ inch long

180-grit sandpaper

Cotton cloth

Marine sealer/varnish,
satin finish

3-inch paintbrush

Tub and tile caulk

*This sink is 13½ inches
in diameter and
5½ inches deep.

WOOD SHOP

Potting Bench Vanity

A POTTING BENCH was the starting point for this charming vanity; marine sealer/varnish made it suitable for a wet area. When choosing a bench, be sure the top surface is deep enough, from front to back, to accommodate a sink and the lower shelf is low enough to allow for the plumbing underneath the sink. Because the bench is likely to be higher than a standard vanity, you may need to consult a plumber.

FINISHED SIZE 48 inches wide, 24 inches deep, 36 inches tall

Cutting the Sink and the Faucet Holes

1 Using the electric driver/drill, remove the back of the potting bench and set it aside.

2 Using the template that comes with the sink, mark a cutting line for the opening with the waterproof marker. Be sure to allow enough room behind the sink for the faucet. (On this bench, the sink was placed as far forward as possible without hitting the front rail underneath.)

3 Cut the hole for the water line with the drill and the hole saw attachment. (The faucet will come with a template for this hole.) When determining where to cut the hole, consider how far the faucet spout will extend over the sink.

4 Using the drill with the ½-inch bit, drill a pilot hole for the jigsaw.

5 Before you cut the sink opening, cover the shelf below to protect it from pieces of falling wood. Starting in the pilot hole, cut out the sink opening using the jigsaw.

TIP

THE MARINE SEALER/VARNISH IS ESSENTIAL TO PROTECT THE BENCH FROM WATER DAMAGE, BUT IT DRIES SLOWLY. ALLOW YOURSELF A TOTAL OF TWO WEEKS' DRYING TIME. PLAN TO WORK ON THE BENCH IN A WELL-VENTILATED ROOM OTHER THAN YOUR BATHROOM SO YOU CAN KEEP YOUR EXISTING SINK FUNCTIONING AS LONG AS POSSIBLE.

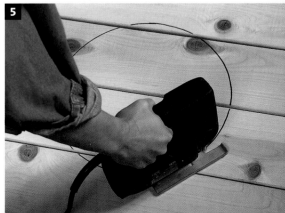

9 Using a bit smaller than the #6 wood screws, predrill a pilot hole through each hole drilled in the previous step and into the brace.

10 Install a wood screw through each hole and into the brace.

11 Put a small amount of wood glue on one end of each wood plug. Insert each plug into a hole. Lightly sand the plugs with the 180-grit sandpaper to make them flush with the rails.

Finishing the Vanity

12 Wipe the bench thoroughly with the cotton cloth to remove any debris. Apply the varnish to all surfaces using the 3-inch brush; allow to dry until it is no longer tacky. Apply a total of four coats to the upper and front surfaces and two coats to the back of the bench.

13 Using the electric driver/drill, reattach the back to the bench.

14 Turn the sink upside down. Run two ¼-inch beads of the caulk around the rim, applying enough to force a little up around the rim when the sink is in place. Set the sink.

15 Set the faucet with caulk.

16 Position the vanity. Hook up the water supply and the drain lines.

Adding the Braces

6 Using the steel tape, measure the distance between the front and back rails on the underside of the bench top. Using the circular saw or the miter box with backsaw, cut two braces to that length from the 1-by-2 lumber.

7 With the 1-inch edge snug against the underside, position a brace on each side of the sink opening, between the rails. Lightly mark guidelines on the outside of the rails to indicate the location of the braces.

8 Using the ½-inch brad-point bit, drill two holes between each pair of guidelines marked in the previous step, drilling them ¼ inch deep (the depth of the wood plugs).

TIP

TO KEEP FROM DRILLING THE HOLE TOO DEEP, WRAP A PIECE OF MASKING TAPE AROUND THE BIT AT A DISTANCE EQUAL TO THE DESIRED HOLE DEPTH.

MATERIALS

Two pieces of 1-by-6 lumber*

⅝-inch half-round molding*

2½-inch crown molding*

Oil-base primer

2½-inch paintbrush

White latex paint, semigloss finish

Brad nailer with ¾- and 1¼-inch nails

Spackling

180-grit sandpaper

Two pieces of ceiling-mount drapery track,* including end stops, and ball-bearing carriers with hooks**
(see Resources, page 142)

Lacquer or clear nail polish (see Step 7)

Electric driver/drill with bits

#6 brass-coated drywall screws, 1½ inches long

Metal file (see Step 9)

Stud finder

Four #8 brass-coated screws, 2½ inches long

Caulk

*Equal in length to the distance to be spanned, less ⅛ inch.

**You'll need one carrier for each ring on the shower curtain and each hole in the liner.

IN A WEEKEND

Curtain Track and Cornice

A CEILING-MOUNTED CORNICE trimmed in molding hides the drapery track and hook carriers for a full-length shower curtain and curtain liner. The track pieces can be ordered the exact length you need through a window-treatment workroom, or you can order standard lengths and cut them with a hacksaw. Extra-long (84-inch) shower curtain liners are available at stores specializing in bath fixtures and accessories.

Assembling the Cornice

1 Prime the 1-by-6 pieces and the molding as follows using the oil-base primer and the 2½-inch paintbrush:
• *both* sides and *both* long edges of one 1-by-6 piece
• *one* side and *both* long edges of the remaining 1-by-6 piece
• the half-round molding and the crown molding.
Allow the pieces to dry thoroughly, at least 1 day. Paint the primed surfaces with the latex paint.

2 Using the brad nailer and ¾-inch nails, attach the half-round molding flush with the lower edge of the 1-by-6 piece that was painted on both sides. Insert the nails straight in, not at an angle, placing them at the ends and approximately 8 inches apart. This piece is the fascia board, the board you see when facing the tub-shower.

3 Fill the nail holes with spackling; let dry, sand, and touch up with the paint.

4 Stand the remaining 1-by-6 piece on the upper edge of the fascia board as shown, with the board edges aligned. Using a pencil, mark a line on the fascia board.

5 Stand the plain board on its edge, with the unpainted side facing away from you. (This side will be mounted against the ceiling.) Align the upper edge of the fascia board with the ceiling board as shown. Nail the fascia board to the ceiling board using the 1¼-inch nails, placing the nails equidistant from the edge and the marked line and every 8 inches down the length of the board.

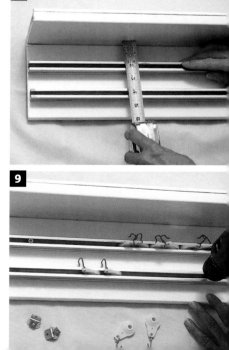

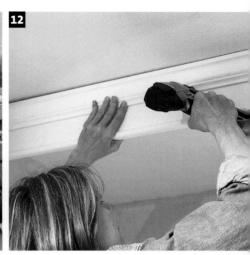

Attaching the Track and the Carriers

6 Turn the cornice over so the unpainted side of the ceiling board is facedown. Place the two pieces of drapery track on the ceiling board, approximately 1½ and 3½ inches from the inner edge, as shown.

7 If the hooks on the carriers are zinc-plated (the packaging will say), coat them with lacquer or clear nail polish to prevent rust.

8 Slide the carriers into the tracks so the hooks face toward the *front* for the fabric curtain (the curtain closest to the fascia board) and toward the *back* for the liner. Insert a stop at each end of each track.

9 Slide the carriers away from the predrilled holes in the tracks. Using the electric driver/drill, predrill through the holes into the ceiling board. Insert a #6 drywall screw partway into each hole, just beyond

the "lips" of the track. (You'll need to press firmly. If necessary, file the lip edges later to allow the carriers to move smoothly.)

Mounting the Cornice

10 Determine where to mount the cornice based on where you want the shower curtain to hang. Use the stud finder to locate the joists in the ceiling (see the tip below). Mark with a pencil just beyond where the ceiling board will be mounted, so you can see the marks when the cornice is held in place for attaching.

> ### TIP
>
> IF THERE ARE NO CEILING JOISTS IN THE RIGHT LOCA-TION, USE MOLLEY BOLTS TO INSTALL THE CORNICE.

11 Have two helpers hold the cornice in place while you predrill a pair of holes near each end of the ceiling board. *Make sure these holes will go into the joists.* Attach the cornice using the #8 screws. Finish screwing in the track screws you installed partway in Step 9.

Finishing the Cornice

12 Using the brad nailer with the ¾-inch nails, attach the crown molding to the upper edge of the cornice, placing the nails at the ends and every 8 inches along the top and bottom of the molding. Fill any gaps between the crown molding and the fascia board with caulk; let dry, sand, and touch up with the paint.

13 Standing in the tub-shower, hang the fabric curtain from the carriers on the outer track. Hang the curtain liner from the carriers on the inner track.

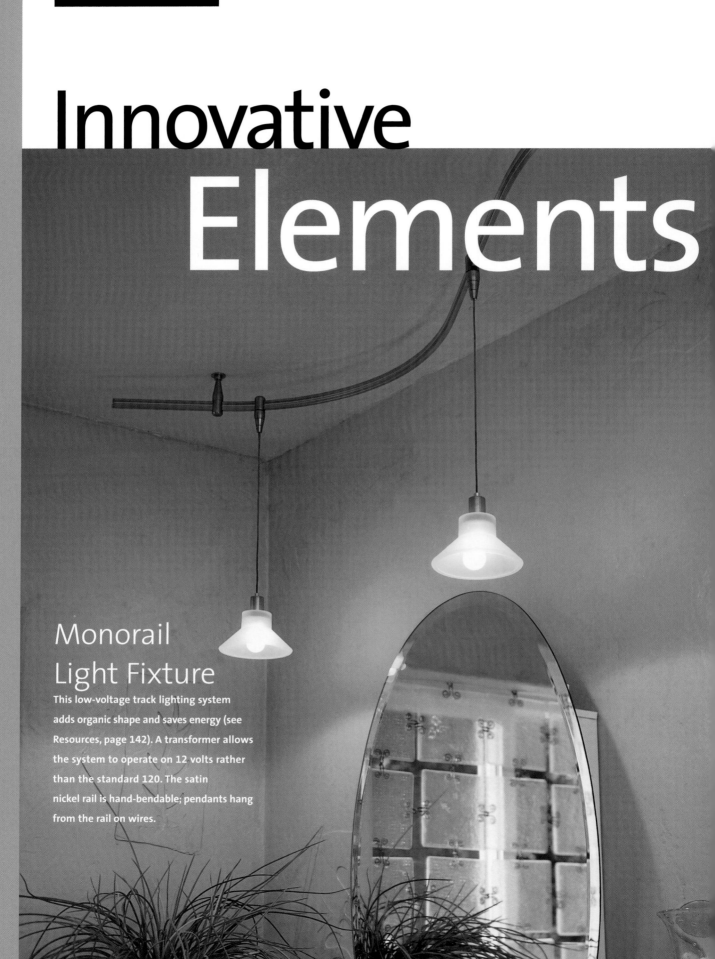

Innovative Elements

Monorail Light Fixture

This low-voltage track lighting system adds organic shape and saves energy (see Resources, page 142). A transformer allows the system to operate on 12 volts rather than the standard 120. The satin nickel rail is hand-bendable; pendants hang from the rail on wires.

Mirrored Cabinet

ABOVE: **Meant to be recessed into the wall, this medicine cabinet (see Resources, page 142) just fits over the back of the bench. The oval mirror introduces a vertical element and visually links the cabinet to the bench.**

Glass "Curtain"

LEFT: **Textured tiles made of recycled glass are joined by copper wires wrapped around hooks embedded in the glass (see Resources, page 142).**

Shower Curtain

**Semisheer fabric in an elegant twining pattern (see Resources, page 142)
reiterates the garden theme and dresses up the bath. The fabric curtain and the
liner both hang from drapery track mounted on the underside of a cornice.**

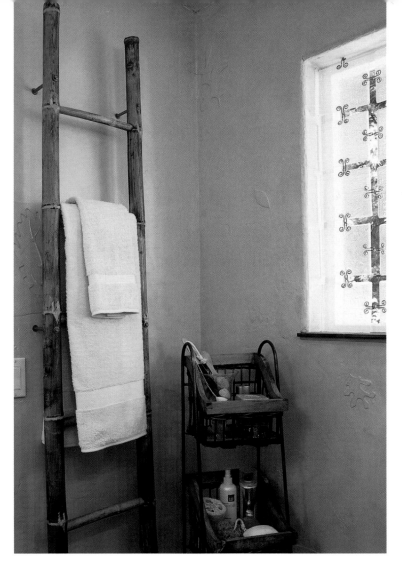

Towel Bar

LEFT: **Bolts installed through the upright pieces and into wall studs turn a bamboo ladder into a towel bar.**

Faucet

BELOW: **A farm-style faucet keeps to the earthy theme. The satin nickel handle repeats the finish of the track light.**

Floor Register

ABOVE: **Holes drilled through two slate tiles replace a standard heating/cooling register. To keep out small objects, a piece of fine screen was laid over the register opening before thinset was applied to the surrounding underlayment.**

Color Splash

BATHED IN COOL BLUES and warm greens, this reinvented bath makes a bright and breezy color statement. Walls papered with plain tissue and painted two shades of sea blue form a textured backdrop for a mosaic mirror frame and other tile accents. The offbeat curtain panel made of vinyl and fabric reiterates the tile shapes and colors on a much larger scale. Lighthearted additions include a white etagere that puts wasted space to use, a paper picture frame (on top of the etagere) in a darker version of the wall color, and milky glass light shades trimmed with leftover tile.

BEFORE: The walls in this remodeled guest bath were a blank canvas just waiting for color. The existing tile counter provided the inspiration.

Steel tape measure

Scissors

Transparent tape

Tear-away stabilizer, available at fabric stores, equal to the finished curtain size, plus 2 inches on each edge*

Cardboard cutting board with 1-inch grid, available at fabric and craft stores

6- by 24-inch acrylic rotary ruler, cutter, and cutting mat, available at fabric stores and quilt shops

Cotton fabrics (see Resources, page 142)

4ml clear vinyl, 54 inches wide, twice the length of the curtain, plus ¼ yard

Clear-drying fabric glue

Pins

Walking foot

Thread to match one of the fabrics

Clip-on curtain rings, one more than the number of squares across

Tension curtain rod

*Stabilizer is only 22 inches wide; you'll need to tape pieces together.

DO IT TODAY

Color Block Curtain

RAW-EDGE SQUARES OF FABRIC sandwiched between two layers of clear, lightweight vinyl appear to float in this easy-to-make curtain panel. A walking-foot attachment for your sewing machine prevents the vinyl from shifting as you sew. Use a shorter-than-average stitch to make it easier to tear away the stabilizer (the foundation material placed under the vinyl) and to keep the threads from raveling at the edges.

FINISHED SIZE 26½ by 26½ inches, with 5-inch fabric squares

1 Measure the width of the window opening with the steel tape. Divide the width by the number of squares desired across the window to find the size of the *grid* squares you will draw on the stabilizer. Decide how many squares long you want the curtain to be. In general, this curtain is most pleasing if it is approximately three-fourths the length of the window.

2 Cut and tape together pieces of the stabilizer to equal the finished curtain size, plus 2 inches on each edge. Tape the stabilizer to your cardboard cutting board. Using the rotary ruler, draw a grid with the desired number of squares across and down, using the grid-square size you determined in Step 1.

3 Using the rotary ruler, cutter, and cutting mat, cut the fabrics into the number of squares needed, making each fabric square *¼ inch smaller* than the grid squares; for example, if the grid squares are 5¼ inches, the fabric squares should be 5 inches.

4 Using scissors, cut the vinyl into two equal pieces, each several inches larger than the grid drawn in Step 2. Lay one piece of vinyl on top of the grid so its edges extend beyond the outer grid lines.

5 Arrange the fabric squares as desired on the grid, over the vinyl.

On each fabric square, put a tiny dot of the fabric glue on the wrong side at the top corners; center each fabric square in its grid square.

6 Carefully lay the second piece of vinyl on top of the fabric squares.

7 Pin through all layers at every other grid-line intersection to minimize the number of pinholes.

8 Attach the walking foot to your machine. Sew on the vertical grid lines, stitching through all layers and starting and stopping ¼ inch beyond the outermost lines; remove the pins just before you reach them. To prevent the curtain from bunching up as you're sewing, turn the curtain around when you get to the middle and stitch from the opposite edge. Repeat on the horizontal grid lines.

9 Working from the back, cut a slit *in the stabilizer only* on each square; gently tear away the stabilizer, square by square.

10 Using the rotary equipment, carefully trim the curtain ⅛ inch *beyond* the outer stitching lines, cutting through both layers of vinyl.

11 Attach a clip-on ring at each vertical line of stitching. Slip the rings onto the tension rod and fit it into the window opening.

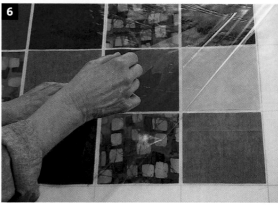

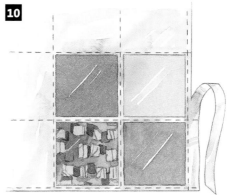

Trimmed edge

MATERIALS

Handmade paper,
at least 10 by 12 inches
(see Resources, page 142)

White 8- by 10-inch
mat precut for a
5- by 7-inch photo

Acrylic rotary ruler,
available at fabric stores
and quilt shops

Small, sharp scissors

Cardboard scrap larger
than the mat

Flat-drying glue

Medium-size craft brush

Clear embossing ink

Clear embossing powder

Heat tool

5- by 7-inch photo

8- by 10-inch
picture-frame back

DO IT TODAY

Paper Picture Frame

EMBOSSING INK, EMBOSSING POWDER, and handmade paper—materials typically used in the craft of stamping—transform a plain picture mat into a one-of-a-kind frame for a favorite photo. Don't be confused by the term "ink." Clear embossing ink is actually a colorless, viscous liquid. All the materials, including the heat tool for melting the powder, are available at art and craft supply stores.

TIP

TO ACHIEVE A DAPPLED

EFFECT, SELECT A PAPER W

OPEN AREAS SO THE WHIT

MAT SHOWS THROUGH.

2

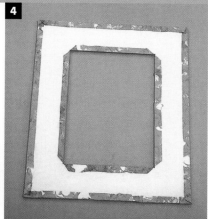

3

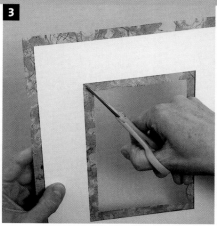

4

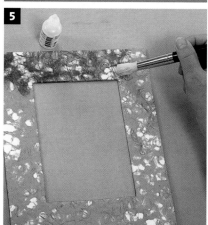

1 Lay the handmade paper right side down. Lay the mat, beveled side down, on top of it. Using the rotary ruler, measure and mark the paper ³/₈ inch beyond the inner and outer edges of the mat. Remove the mat and cut the paper along the lines using the scissors.

2 Lay the cardboard scrap on your work surface; lay the art paper right side down on the cardboard. Using your fingers, apply glue evenly to the right side of the mat. Center the mat, right side down, on the paper; press to adhere.

3 Working from the wrong side of the mat, snip the paper into each inner corner at a 45-degree angle.

4 Still working on the wrong side, apply glue liberally along the inner and outer edges of the mat. Fold the paper's edges to the wrong side and adhere them to the mat. Allow the glue to dry.

5 Turn the mat right side up. Using the brush, apply the embossing ink generously to the surface. Work quickly so the ink does not dry.

6 Immediately sprinkle embossing powder over the mat, striving for an even coating.

7 Turn on the heat tool and allow it to warm up for a few seconds. Holding the tool straight up and down a few inches from the paper, begin to melt the embossing powder. As soon as the powder dissolves and turns shiny, move the heat tool to the next area. Watch carefully; the powder will scorch if it gets too hot.

8 On the front of the photo, apply a dot of glue to each corner; adhere the photo to the wrong side of the mat. Allow the glue to dry. Glue the picture-frame back to the back of the mat.

5

6

7

MATERIALS

Steel tape measure

Wide, clear tape

Surface bullnose tile, enough to frame the upper and side edges of the window casing, plus 1 linear foot*

Radius bullnose tile, two pieces*

Blue painter's tape

Snap cutter or wet saw, available at tile stores (see Step 6)

Small ruler

Rubber or latex gloves

$^3/_{16}$- by $^1/_4$-inch V-notched trowel

Mastic (adhesive)

Fine felt-tip pen, in a color slightly darker than the tile

White premixed grout

Grout float

Tile sponge

Cotton cloth

*These tiles were originally 4 inches square. See Resources, page 142.

IN A WEEKEND

Tile Surround

A BAND OF CERAMIC TILE sets off the wood casing around the window and visually links the tiled vanity to the window wall. Determining the width to cut the tiles so they fit perfectly around the casing takes a bit of experimentation; be patient and double-check your measurements. Use a high-quality snap cutter to get the cleanest possible cuts. You can also rent a wet saw from a tile supplier to make the cuts; ask for instructions.

Calculating the Cut Width

1 Using the steel tape, measure the width of the window casing along the upper edge. Lightly mark the midpoint with a pencil.

2 Using the clear tape, join enough surface bullnose pieces to go across the window casing, with equal spacing of ⅛ to ¼ inch between tiles and an overhang on each side of approximately one-half tile. Make sure the rounded edges of the tiles are on top.

3 Precisely center the tile strip on the casing. Tape it to the wall using the painter's tape. Measure the length of the strip. Note whether the midpoint falls at the center of a tile or between two tiles (see Step 11).

4 From the length of the strip, subtract the width of the window casing; divide by 2. This measurement should equal the width of the overhang on each side. It is also the width you'll need to cut the tiles in order to create a continuous, uniform band around the window.

Cutting and Setting the Tile

5 Remove the strip and untape the tile. Refer to the illustration at right as you measure and mark the tile for cutting. Pay particular attention to the corner pieces, making sure the bullnose edges and corners

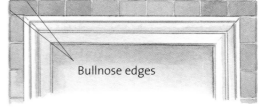

Bullnose edges

are facing out. Wait until Step 14 to cut the bottom piece on each side.

6 Cut the tile using the snap cutter or the wet saw, following the manufacturer's instructions. (If you use a wet saw, wear eye and ear protection.)

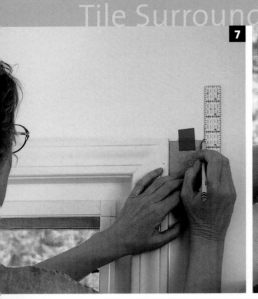

7 Tape a cut surface bullnose piece so it's snug against the top right edge of the casing, with the bullnose edge facing out. Mark the wall at the outer edge of the tile; extend the line upward using the ruler. Repeat on the left side of the window casing. You'll use these marks to set the corner pieces.

8 Wearing gloves and using the V-notched trowel, "back-butter" the radius bullnose piece for the upper-right corner with the mastic. Wipe away excess mastic on the edges with a paper towel.

9 Set the piece on the upper edge of the casing as shown, aligning the right edge with the line drawn in Step 7. Press the tile to the wall.

10 Repeat to set the remaining radius bullnose piece at the upper-left corner .

11 If the midpoint of the tile strip will fall at the *center* of a tile, as it did on this casing, measure and lightly mark that point on the cut edge of a surface bullnose tile, using the felt-tip pen. Back-butter and set the piece, aligning the mark on the tile with the midpoint marked on the casing. If the midpoint of the strip will fall *between* two tiles, back-butter and set a tile just to the right of the midpoint marked on the casing, at a distance of approximately one-half the spacing between tiles.

12 Set surface bullnose pieces from the center to the right corner piece, eyeballing the spacing between the tiles. Set surface bullnose pieces to the left corner piece.

13 Set pieces down the right and left sides of the casing, maintaining equal spacing.

14 When you get to the bottom on each side, measure the space between the last full tile and the windowsill, allowing space for grout between the last full tile and the bottom piece. Measure, mark, and cut a tile to fit; set it so the just-cut edge is at the bottom, resting on the sill, and the bullnose edge is facing out. Allow the mastic to cure according to the manufacturer's instructions.

Grouting the Tile

15 Mask off the wall with painter's tape to protect it from the grout. Stir the premixed grout thoroughly. Apply with a grout float, working it firmly into the spaces.

16 With the tile sponge moistened and then wrung nearly dry, wipe the excess grout off the surface; rinse the sponge often. When a haze forms, wipe the tile with the cotton cloth. Allow the grout to dry according to the manufacturer's instructions; carefully remove the tape.

MATERIALS

1- by ½-inch molding totaling perimeter of plywood, plus several feet

½-inch plywood, 26 by 30 inches

Miter box with backsaw

Wood glue

Brad nailer with 1-inch nails

Spackling

180-grit sandpaper

2-inch paintbrush

Latex primer

Mirror, 20 by 24 inches, available at home centers

Epoxy cement

IN A WEEKEND

Mosaic Mirror

A BEVELED MIRROR SURROUNDED BY GLASS TILE adds rich color and lively pattern to this small bath. Half-inch plywood framed by plain molding provides the foundation for the mosaic work. This project uses both ¾-inch opaque glass tile designed for nipping into small pieces and 1-inch translucent glass tile. Special tile adhesive, grout, and tools make the project easy for the beginner. Because the tile adhesive must cure 24 hours, the project may take you more than 2 days.

FINISHED SIZE

26¾ by 30¾ inches

Step by Step

Assembling the Frame

1 Set a 1-inch edge of the molding strip against one edge of the plywood and mark the strip at one end for a miter cut. Cut the strip using the miter box with backsaw. Set the strip against the edge of the plywood, with the mitered end at one corner. Mark the miter cut at the other end of the strip; cut.

2 Run a bead of wood glue along the inside edge of the molding piece. Adhere the piece to the edge of the plywood, flush with the back.

3 Using the brad nailer and the 1-inch nails, nail the molding to the plywood at the corners and approximately every 6 inches. Mark, cut, glue, and nail the remaining pieces of molding.

4 Apply spackling to fill any gaps at the corners; allow to dry. Sand with the 180-grit sandpaper.

TIP BECAUSE THE EDGES OF THE TILE ARE ROUNDED OR BEVELED, THE SPACING BETWEEN PIECES WILL APPEAR WIDER ONCE YOU APPLY THE GROUT. ERR ON THE SIDE OF CLOSER PLACEMENT, BUT DON'T LET THE TILES TOUCH. YOU MIGHT WANT TO DO A SMALL PRACTICE PIECE TO DETERMINE THE SPACING YOU LIKE.

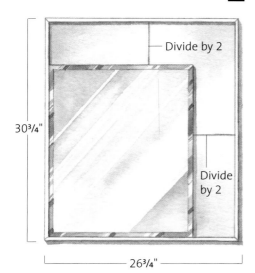

6

30³/4"

Divide by 2

Divide by 2

26³/4"

5 Using the 2-inch brush, prime the plywood and the molding with the latex primer; allow to dry.

Gluing the Mirror to the Frame

6 Set the mirror in the plywood frame and push it into the lower-left corner as shown above. Measure the gaps at the top and the right side; divide each by 2 to arrive at the spacing required to center the mirror in the frame.

7 Carefully center the mirror and draw around the edges with a pencil.

8 Remove the mirror. Following the manufacturer's instructions, apply the epoxy cement to the ply-wood within the drawn lines; adhere the mirror.

9 Center the 18- by 22-inch piece of paper on the front of the mirror. Tape the paper to the mirror with the blue painter's tape, placing the tape precisely at—not over—the mirror edges.

Setting the Tile

10 Do a dry-run placement of a few tiles to get a feel for how the pieces will fit within the frame.

11 Wearing the gloves, use the spreader to comb a thin layer of tile adhesive on a small area.

12 Set the tiles in the adhesive. It's easiest to start with an orderly arrangement, then work into a more free-form pattern. Add an occasional floral marble.

13 Using the nippers, cut tiles to create fill-in pieces. The ¾-inch tile shown here has small ridges running in one direction on the right side. For the cleanest cuts on ridged tile, place the nippers at the edge of a tile, against a ridge and parallel to the other ridges; close the nippers with firm, even pressure. Always nip tile inside a heavyweight, reclosable

7

10

11

13

12

plastic bag to protect yourself from slivers of glass.

14 Finish setting tiles and marbles all the way around the mirror. Allow the adhesive to cure 24 hours.

Grouting the Tile

15 Tape the top and inside edges of the molding with painter's tape. Mix the grout in the plastic bucket according to the manufacturer's instructions. Load the float side of the float/sponge with a generous dollop of grout.

16 Spread the grout over the tile, working at an angle and pushing the grout firmly between the pieces. Strive to keep the grout on the same level as the edge of the mirror, not above it.

17 Allow the grout to set up 10 minutes. Moisten the float/sponge and wring it nearly dry. Gently wipe the excess grout from the tile surface, rinsing the sponge often.

18 When a haze forms on the tile, gently wipe the surface with the clean cotton cloth.

Finishing the Mirror

19 Remove the tape from the top and inside edges of the molding. Protect the tiled area next to the molding with painter's tape. Using

the 1-inch brush, paint the frame edges with two coats of latex paint, allowing the paint to dry between coats. Remove the tape. Also remove the tape and the paper covering the mirror.

20 Attach the mirror hanging hardware to the back. Using the stud finder, determine whether the desired placement of the mirror falls over a wall stud. To hang the mirror as flat as possible on drywall, use nylon anchors in combination with the appropriate screws, rather than the projecting hooks that often come in mirror hanging kits. Be sure to drill pilot holes for the anchors before screwing them into the wall. To mount the mirror into a stud, use wood screws instead of nylon anchors and screws.

Light Fixture

INSTALLING A NEW LIGHT FIXTURE is a simple task that requires only basic tools. The following instructions are general; almost all fixtures will come with detailed directions. Before you begin, turn off the power at the circuit breaker or fuse box. Remove the existing fixture and disconnect the wiring from it. The majority of electrical boxes will have wires like the ones you see here; if the wiring in your box looks different, consult an electrician.

MATERIALS

Light fixture, including mounting plate, hardware, and wire nuts

Phillips screwdriver

Flathead screwdriver

Wire strippers

Pliers

Electrical tape

Carpenter's level

Glass tile
(see Resources, page 142)

Resin beads

Nonflammable tile adhesive (see Resources, page 142)

1 From the back of the new mounting plate, insert one screw at the top and one screw at the bottom. (These screws will protrude outward.) Fit the mounting plate over the electrical box, with the wires coming through the opening as shown. Using the Phillips screwdriver, attach the mounting plate to the electrical box with two more screws, putting one screw at the left and one at the right, through the curved slots in the mounting plate. (The slots allow you to level the fixture once it's attached to the plate.)

2 Wrap the copper grounding wire coming from the electrical box around the green grounding screw on the mounting plate. Use the flat-head screwdriver to prevent the screw from turning.

3 Strip ¾ inch of insulation from the ends of the black (power) and white (neutral) wires that extend from the electrical box and the back of the fixture. Holding the black wires parallel, twist the stripped ends together with the pliers; join the white wires in the same way. Also twist together the end of the copper wire wrapped around the grounding screw and the end of the copper wire coming from the fixture.

4 Cap the twisted wires by screwing on the wire nuts provided. Use the smaller one (yellow in this example) for the grounding wires, which are smaller, and the larger ones for the black and white wires.

5 To prevent the wire nuts from loosening when you push them

back into the electrical box, wrap the base of each with electrical tape, wrapping in the same direction as you screwed on the nuts.

6 Gently push the wires into the electrical box.

7 Fit the fixture over the screws that protrude from the mounting plate. Screw on the cap nuts to secure the fixture to the plate.

8 Use the carpenter's level to check the alignment of the fixture. To adjust it, remove the cap nuts, loosen the mounting screws at left and right, and adjust the plate.

9 Glue glass tiles and resin beads to the edges of the shades using the tile adhesive. Install the shades.

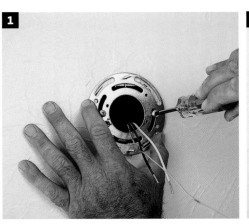

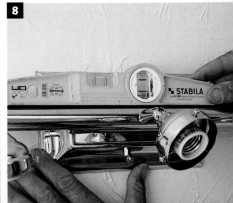

Paper-and-Paint Walls

WHITE TISSUE PAPER AND WALLPAPER PASTE are the secret ingredients in this simple wall treatment. The crinkly effect comes from manipulating the tissue on the walls while the paste is still wet. Choosing the paint colors is a snap: select a color for the light background, then count down two hues on the same paint strip for the slightly darker "shadow" color.

MATERIALS

4-inch paintbrush

All-purpose wallpaper paste

White tissue paper totaling the square footage of the walls, plus 10 percent

Latex primer

Latex paint in two colors* (see Resources, page 142)

Latex glazing medium*

Plastic bowl

Paint stir sticks

2½-inch paintbrush

Tile sponge

Soft cotton cloths

*For a small bathroom, you'll need 1 gallon of the lighter-color paint, 1 quart of the darker-color paint, and 1 quart of the glazing medium.

Applying the Tissue

1 Using the 4-inch brush, apply a thin coat of wallpaper paste over an area slightly larger than a piece of the tissue.

2 Loosely place the first piece of tissue over the pasted area, keeping it approximately straight.

3 As you adhere the tissue to the wall, manipulate it with your hands to create tiny wrinkles. Don't be concerned if the tissue tears; blend any torn edges with additional wall-paper paste.

4 Brush on more paste adjacent to the first sheet. Adhere the second piece, overlapping the first sheet by approximately 1½ inches.

5 Where a noticeable wrinkle occurs in the first sheet of tissue, sculpt the second sheet with your hands so the wrinkle appears to continue across the seam.

TIP

IF YOU CAN'T SEE THE PASTE ON THE WALLS IN STEP 1, SHINE A LIGHT ON IT FROM THE SIDE; THE WET PASTE WILL GLISTEN.

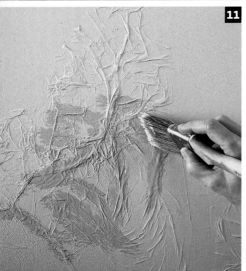

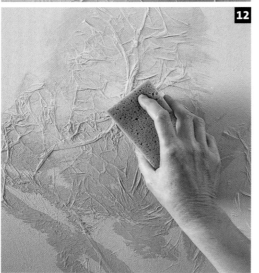

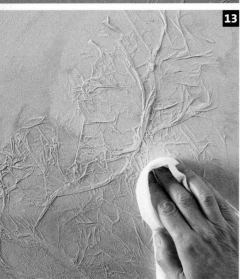

pool in the creases of the tissue. Allow the primer to dry.

9 With a minimum of the lighter paint on the brush, paint the walls, brushing in the direction of the wrinkles and being careful not to let the paint pool in the creases. Allow to dry.

10 Combine approximately ½ cup of the darker paint and 1 cup of the glazing medium in the plastic bowl. Mix to blend with a paint stir stick.

11 Using the 2½-inch brush, dab the paint-glazing mixture over the wrinkles. Work in a 2-foot-square area, then proceed immediately to the next step.

12 Moisten the tile sponge and wring it nearly dry. Lightly go over the painted area with the sponge in a sweeping motion, striving to lift some of the darker paint off the ridges of the wrinkles, while keeping some in the creases to create "shadows." Avoid creating conspicuous stop-and-start lines.

13 Using a cloth, dampened slightly, quickly lift a little of the darker color from the flat areas, blending it toward the wrinkles. Rinse the cloth often; replace as needed.

14 Repeat Steps 11 through 13 to complete the walls, mixing more paint and glazing medium as needed.

6 Brush paste lightly over the seam, following the wrinkles.

7 Continue pasting sheets of tissue paper until the walls are covered. Allow to dry overnight.

Painting the Walls

8 Using the 4-inch brush, prime the walls with the latex primer. Work in the direction of the wrinkles, being careful not to let the primer

Practical Purposes

Etagere

ABOVE: **A multilevel, freestanding storage piece with chrome towel hooks adds height to the scheme and disguises the standard shower stall.**

Cabinet

LEFT: **A white cottage cabinet with glass doors looks altogether different with the beadboard back painted the color of the mosaic mirror frame. (The back was easy to unscrew and remove.) Inexpensive wood knobs painted to match the interior replaced the original glass ones.**

111

Classic Appeal

NATURAL MATERIALS AND NEUTRAL COLORS predominate in this ambitious reinvention. Tumbled stone tile covers the countertop and lines the newly created shower; mosaic trim pieces form the vanity backsplash and accent the shower walls. Sheet vinyl flooring resembling bronze-colored concrete "grounds" the room in darker color and adds another visual texture to the scheme. Painting the walls in pale stripes makes a soft backdrop for a collection of decorative fixtures and features. Timeless glass block brings natural light deep into the room while ensuring privacy.

BEFORE: A basic bath with a combination tub-shower was functional, but the homeowners longed for a walk-in shower and a Tuscan look.

Glass Block Window

BOTH A WINDOW AND A WINDOW TREATMENT, glass block affords light and privacy. Keep in mind the following limitations: Glass block is suitable only for non–load bearing windows of 25 square feet or less. In addition, it's not practical for a second story because you'll need to work on the outside as well as the inside. The window opening must be a size divisible by the size of the blocks, plus ¼ inch on all edges. Most manufacturers include an instruction booklet and offer a how-to video.

Preparing the Opening

Because the window opening must be sized to fit the blocks, you will probably need to reframe the window, as was done in this shower. Have a general contractor prepare the opening and the walls; if you plan to tile the shower, make sure the contractor allows for the thickness of the tile when sizing the window. The following photos show water-proof building paper wrapped around the inside of the window frame and multiboard on the walls.

Attaching the Perimeter Channels

1 Using the handsaw, cut a piece of perimeter channel to fit the sill. (Drill new holes at the ends if the predrilled holes get cut off.) Attach the channel piece to the sill using the #6 zinc-plated screws. Cut the side channel pieces to rest on the sill piece, leaving space for the upper channel piece. Screw the side channel pieces to the window frame.

2 Cut the upper channel piece to the length required. Using the utility knife, cut the piece in half lengthwise. Slip one half into the back of the window opening and screw it to the frame, as shown. Set aside the remaining half.

3 Paint the screw heads with the white craft paint; allow to dry.

Setting the Blocks

4 Using the margin trowel and the mortar pan, mix the first batch of mortar according to the manu-facturer's instructions, carefully noting the precautions. It's best to mix approximately one-fourth bag of mortar at a time to prevent it from drying out as you work. (After it's mixed with water, the mortar has an "open time" of approximately 1 hour.) The mortar should adhere to the side of a block when it's held upright. Be sure to test the mortar on a block before proceeding; add water or powder and remix if needed.

5 Set the first block, without any mortar, in the lower-left corner of the perimeter channel, as shown below. The block will fit snugly within the channel. Set another block in the lower-right corner.

6 Return to the left side of the window opening. Using the margin trowel, "butter" the left edge of another block with a ³⁄₈- to ¹⁄₂-inch layer of mortar.

TIP

AS YOU SET BLOCKS, CHECK TO SEE THAT EACH JOINT IS FILLED COMPLETELY WITH MORTAR. IF IT'S NOT, USE THE FOAM BRUSH TO FILL VOIDS WITH ADDITIONAL MORTAR.

7 Set the block snug against the first block. Insert a regular spacer (see "Glass Block Spacers" above right) between the blocks as shown. These blocks were photographed with minimal mortar to show the spacers clearly; you will need to use more.

8 Butter and set the next block snug against the previous block in the same way. Insert a regular spacer between the blocks. Continue working to the right.

Glass Block Spacers

Take a close look at the spacers. They feature "toothed legs," "smooth arms," and a "crossbar." You'll need to modify some of the spacers as follows:

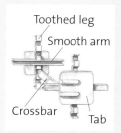

Regular Spacer

- When instructed to insert a "regular" spacer, use the spacer as is, with the crossbar *down*.
- At each end of each row, you'll need to insert a "flat" spacer between the block and the perimeter channel. To make a flat spacer, orient a regular spacer as shown and cut off the smooth arms with the wire cutters. Use the rasp to file the cut edges all the way down to the toothed legs. (This step is essential to ensure accurate block spacing.)

Flat Spacer

- When installing the next-to-the-last row, you'll need both flat and "H" spacers. To make an H spacer, cut off the upper toothed leg and *half* of the tab on the near side (the side facing the room). Insert the H spacers where you would use regular spacers on the next-to-the-last row.

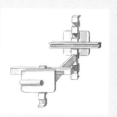

H Spacer

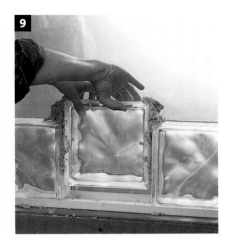

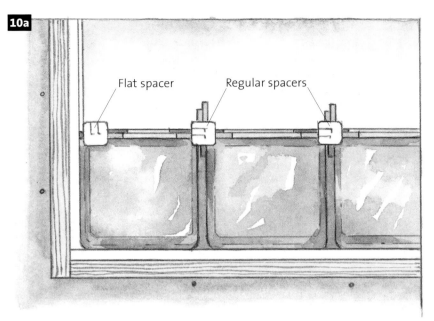

Flat spacer   Regular spacers

9 For the last block (it will be second from the end), butter both edges. Slide the block into place; some mortar will come out on the sides and the top. Insert regular spacers between the blocks.

10 At each end of the row, insert a flat spacer, with the ridges on the tabs pointing up (see the photo and the illustration).

11 Once the first row is set, spread the tops of the blocks with mortar. Be careful not to get mortar on the smooth arms of the spacers; if you do, wipe it off or the spacing will be inaccurate and the top row won't fit.

12 Install the second row in the same manner, setting each corner block without mortar. For each subsequent block, butter the left edge, set the block in the spacers, and insert a regular spacer on top.

13 Butter both edges of the last block; insert. At each end of the second row, insert a flat spacer.

14 Check the second row with the carpenter's level. If the blocks are not level, use the rubber mallet to gently work them into place.

15 Also check each vertical row, placing the level against the blocks to make sure they aren't too far forward or back. If necessary, remove blocks, reapply mortar, and reset.

16 Spread mortar on the top of the second row, again being careful not to cover the smooth arms of the spacers with mortar.

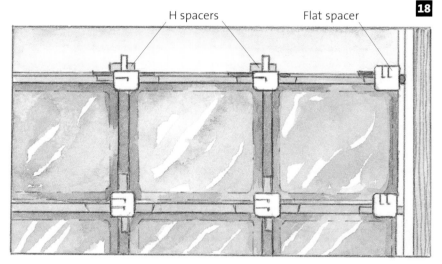

H spacers   Flat spacer

17 Set the third row as you did the second. Be sure to check the blocks, horizontally and vertically, with the level. Continue working up the window opening, placing the appropriate spacer after setting each block and checking each row with the level.

18 As you set the next-to-the-last row, use H spacers between blocks where you would normally place regular spacers (see the illustration above left). Use flat spacers at the ends as you did on previous rows.

19 Set the top row, placing the corner blocks first. These blocks are more difficult to fit into the channel—be patient and gently work them into place. The last block will be snug.

20 Using the foam brush, fill any gaps between the blocks with mortar.

21 Let the mortar set up 1 hour, then twist off the spacer tabs on both sides of the window. Moisten the tile sponge and wring it nearly dry. Wipe off excess mortar from both sides of the blocks; rinse and wring out the sponge frequently.

22 "Striking" packs mortar into the joints for a moisture-proof seal. Using the striking tool and moderate pressure, pack the horizontal joints first, followed by the vertical ones, as shown. Carefully wipe off the excess mortar. Repeat on the outside of the window.

23 Once the mortar is dry, dampen a cloth and wipe off the haze on the surface of the blocks. For stubborn spots, use a little white vinegar on the cloth.

Finishing the Window

24 Using the utility knife, cut the foam expansion strips lengthwise to 1½ inches wide. Insert the strips, cutting and butting the ends as needed, above the top row of blocks.

25 Insert the remaining half of the upper perimeter channel, cut in Step 2, between the expansion strip and the window frame (the fit will be very snug).

26 Run a bead of clear silicone sealant around the perimeter of the window on the inside and the outside to seal the blocks to the channel.

MATERIALS

4-inch stone tile,
4- by 12-inch mosaic
trim, and 1-inch sheet-
mounted stone tile
(see Resources, page 142)

Wedge spacers, super size

1-by-2 lumber pieces to
encircle the shower
walls, plus one piece

Permanent marker
and carpenter's pencil

Carpenter's level

Electric driver/drill
with bits and hole saw
attachment

#8 zinc-coated screws for
drywall, $1^5/_8$ inches long

Margin trowel and
square-notched trowel*

Thinset adhesive

Rubber or latex gloves

Eye and ear protection

Wet saw and
honing stone

Tile nippers

6-foot lipped straightedge

Blue painter's tape

Sanded grout and
grout float

Tile sponge

Stone and grout sealer

*Ask the tile supplier
to recommend
the best trowels.

MAKEOVER MAGIC

Tumbled Stone Shower

ALTHOUGH IT LOOKS DAUNTING, tiling a shower is a doable project, provided you have help from professionals at crucial points. Before you can tile, a general contractor and a plumber must prepare the shower. You'll also need a tile installer to prepare the shower pan and liner and, after the walls are tiled, to set the shower floor. The part you can do yourself—tiling the walls, windowsill, and surround—is made easier by the natural variations in tumbled stone, which disguise less-than-perfect workmanship.

Making a Plan

1 Plan to begin setting tile just above the shower pan. You'll also need to plan the mosaic-trim placement. In this shower the trim pieces are positioned approximately three-fifths of the way up the window opening.

2 Natural stone has an "A" side and a "B" side; examine your tile to determine which side you want facing out ("A"). Lay out several rows of tile on your work surface, with wedge spacers placed thin edge down between tiles. Choose a straight (be sure to check it) 1-by-2 strip to make a "jury stick." Lay it next to a row of tile and, using the permanent marker, make a mark on the strip at each spacer to represent the grout line between tiles. You'll use the jury stick in Step 4 to determine exactly where to start the first row of tile.

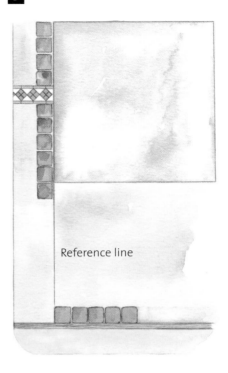

Reference line

Attaching the Furring Strips

3 Using the carpenter's pencil and level, mark a vertical reference line from the lower-left corner of the window down to the shower floor (see the illustration).

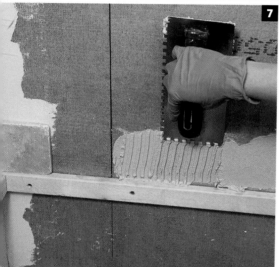

4 Hold the jury stick along the vertical reference line, aligning a tick mark at the lower-left corner of the window. On the multiboard, mark the bottom of the first row of tile that will occur *above* the shower-pan liner.

5 Using the pencil and the level, draw a horizontal line at this point on the multiboard, continuing the line onto all the shower walls. Attach the 1-by-2 furring strips to the multiboard with the #8 screws every 8 inches, aligning the upper edges of the strips with the horizontal line.

Setting the Tile

6 Using the margin trowel, mix a small batch of thinset according to the manufacturer's instructions. Wearing the gloves and holding the straight end of the notched trowel at a 30-degree angle, spread a horizontal band of thinset onto the multiboard. (In the photo, a tile rests in the corner on the furring strip to help determine how high to apply the thinset.)

7 Using the notched end of the trowel, comb the thinset vertically. Leave a small gap in the thinset to allow you to see the reference line.

8 Place the first tile with its lower edge resting on the furring strip and its left edge next to, but not touching, the vertical reference line. "Smoosh" the tile into the adhesive to set it.

9 Set tile to the right, placing wedge spacers between tiles. Continue working toward the corner until you must cut a tile to fit at the end.

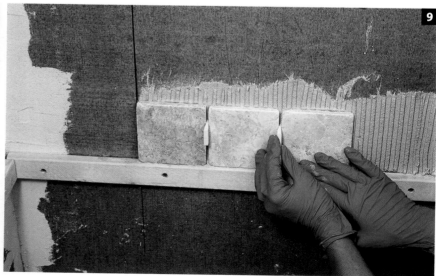

Cutting Tiles

10 To mark the end tile for cutting, stack it precisely on top of the last-set tile. Carefully position another tile in the corner so it rests on top of the stacked tile. Using the side edge of the uppermost tile as a straightedge, mark a cutting line on the stacked tile.

11 Wearing the gloves and the eye and ear protection, cut the tile on the wet saw. Smooth and round the cut edge with the honing stone.

12 Set the end tile so the cut edge is snug in the corner; place a spacer between the end tile and the next-to-last tile.

13 Set the tile to the opposite corner, cutting the end tile to fit.

14 Spread and comb a band of thinset above the first row and set the second row, adding spacers between the tiles and the rows and cutting the end pieces to fit. Check the second row with the level. Remove and reset tiles if needed.

15 Continue working up the wall to the sill, checking the tiles both horizontally and vertically with the level and adjusting tiles as necessary.

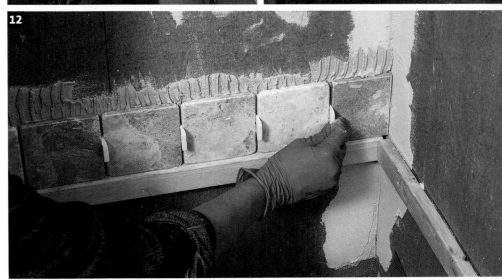

16 Using the level and the 6-foot lipped straightedge, extend the vertical reference line above the window opening.

Tiling the Sill and the Jamb

17 The sill and jamb tile must extend out far enough to be flush with the wall tile. To accurately mark the pieces for cutting, rest a tile on the sill. Holding a loose tile on the already-set wall tile, mark the sill tile at the back edge of the loose tile. Because stone is so irregular, it's a good idea to also hold a loose tile on the opposite side of the sill tile and mark that edge; connect the two marks for a cutting line.

18 Cut the tile on the wet saw. Set the fence on the saw and cut as many additional sill and jamb pieces as needed.

19 Comb thinset on the sill and set a tile in the corner, with the cut edge toward the window.

20 Set the remaining sill tiles, placing wedge spacers between them. Cut the end piece to fit. Set the jamb tile from the sill up, using blue painter's tape and spacers to keep the tiles from slipping.

21 Return to setting tiles up the wall. When you reach the point where you want the mosaic trim to begin, follow the general instructions for "Setting the Backsplash," pages 128 and 129. Set tile on the remaining walls. To cut tile to accommodate the shower handle, see "Cutting Curved Tile," page 127. Use the hole saw attachment to cut the tile around the showerhead.

Setting the Final Tiles

22 Set the shower dam tile, cutting the pieces to fit as needed (see the photo on page 120).

23 Remove the furring strips below the first row. Apply thinset and set the tiles below, all the way to the shower floor, adding spacers between tiles and rows. Cut the tile to fit as needed for the bottom row.

24 Allow the tile to cure 48 hours.

25 Have the professional tile installer set the sheet tile on the shower floor.

Grouting and Sealing the Tile

26 Mix the grout according to the manufacturer's instructions. Holding the float at a slight angle, as shown, push the grout between the tiles, working in all directions and packing the grout as firmly as

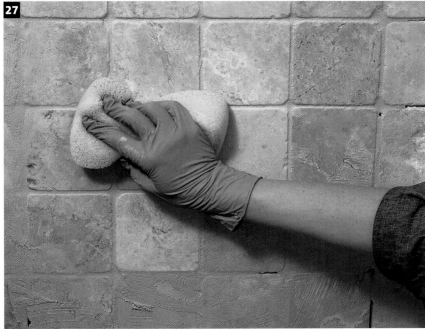

possible until it is flush with the surface of the tile.

27 Moisten the tile sponge and wring it nearly dry. Wipe away the excess grout in a circular motion; rinse the sponge often. Continue

wiping until the haze is gone. Allow the grout to cure at least 48 hours.

28 Apply the sealer according to the manufacturer's instructions, using the recommended cloth.

MATERIALS

Thinset adhesive

Square-notched trowel and notched margin trowel

Kraft paper

Blue painter's tape

Trisodium phosphate

60-grit sandpaper

Steel tape measure

1-by-2 strip equal in length to the vanity width

4-inch stone tile and 4- by 12-inch mosaic trim (see Resources, page 142)

Wedge spacers, super size

Metal straightedge

Carpenter's square

Eye and ear protection

Heavyweight rubber or latex gloves

Wet saw

Tile nippers

Carpenter's level

Honing stone

Small carpenter's square

Masking paper

Sanded grout and grout float

Tile sponge

Stone and grout sealer

IN A WEEKEND

Tumbled Stone Vanity

TILING A VANITY COUNTERTOP over existing tile is a real time-saver; see Step 3 to determine if your vanity is a candidate. Because "nipping" tiles around the sink openings leaves uneven edges, this project is suitable only for a vanity with self-rimming sinks. You'll need to rent a wet saw to make the cuts; be sure to ask for instructions. For the backsplash, you will probably need to cut the mosaic trim pieces to turn each corner. Double-check your measurements before cutting.

Preparing the Surface

1 Remove the sinks and fixtures. If any damage occurs during removal, such as pieces of tile coming loose, mix a small batch of thinset and, using the straight edge of the square-notched trowel, fill the voids to the level of the existing tile. Allow to dry overnight.

2 Tape kraft paper to the front of the cabinets with blue painter's tape below the area you plan to tile.

3 Wash the existing surface with trisodium phosphate to remove any oils; allow to dry. Mix a small batch of thinset and comb on a little using the square-notched trowel; allow to dry overnight. If the thinset adheres to the surface, you can proceed. (First chip off the test thinset with the straight edge of the trowel.) If the thinset comes off easily, you'll need to rough up the surface with 60-grit sandpaper.

Establishing Reference Lines

4 Using the steel tape and a marker, measure and mark the midpoint along the front edge of the vanity.

5 Mark the 1-by-2 strip to make a "jury stick" (see Step 2, "Tumbled Stone Shower," page 121). Use the jury stick to determine whether to center a tile on the midpoint or to set tiles on either side of the midpoint,

as was done here. The goal is to have the largest possible cut pieces at the ends.

6 The first row of counter tile must overhang the front edge a distance equal to the thickness of the tile. To mark a horizontal reference line for this row, hold a tile against the face of the cabinet, even with the upper edge of the counter. Lay another tile on the counter so its front edge is flush with the surface of the face tile. Make a mark on the counter at the back edge of the counter tile. Measure the distance from the mark to the front edge of the vanity. Using this measurement and the metal straightedge, draw a horizontal line on the counter parallel to the front edge. Using the carpenter's square, draw a vertical reference line from the midpoint marked in Step 4 to the back. (See the illustration below.)

Cutting Curved Tile

7 Using the reference lines, lay out as many full tiles as possible on the counter, adding wedge spacers (thin edge down) between tiles. Where a tile extends into a sink opening, mark the curve.

8 Put on the eye and ear protection and the gloves. On the wet saw, cut the tiles that go around the sink openings, making straight cuts 1/8 inch apart toward the curve marked on each tile, as shown.

9 Using the tile nippers, break off the slivers of stone. Nip away at the remaining stone, all the way to the marked curve. Don't be too concerned about perfect curves; the sink rims will cover the cuts.

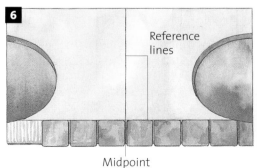

Reference lines

Midpoint

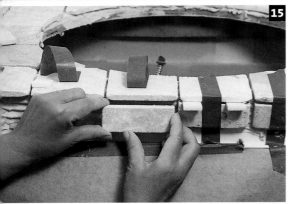

Setting the Tile

10 Remove the tiles in preparation for spreading the adhesive. Load the square-notched trowel with thinset and turn it upside down. If the adhesive runs, the mixture is too loose; if it adheres to the trowel and does not sag, it's ready to spread. Holding the straight edge of the trowel at a 30-degree angle, spread thinset on the counter. Using the narrow notched edge of the trowel, comb the thinset toward the front edge.

11 Set the first row of tile as planned, starting at the midpoint and working toward the ends. Align the back edges of the tiles with the horizontal reference line and place spacers between tiles. Use the carpenter's level to check the surface; if it's not level, pry up the offending tiles, scrape off or add a little thinset, and reset.

12 Measure, mark, and cut the last piece at each end. Set each piece.

13 Set the remaining rows from front to back, using wedge spacers between tiles and rows and cutting

pieces to fit against the wall at the sides and the back.

14 Determine the ideal height for the face tiles, based on the design of the cabinet front. Measure, mark, and cut the tiles on the wet saw. Smooth the just-cut edges with the honing stone, rounding them to match the tumbled edges.

15 Using the 60-grit sandpaper, roughen the area on the cabinet front where the face tile will be set. Spread and comb on the thinset horizontally using the margin trowel. Set the face tile under the counter tile, with the cut edges down. Insert spacers between the counter and face tiles as shown; use blue painter's tape to keep the pieces from slipping. Cut the end pieces to fit; set. Use a level to make sure the face tile is straight up and down, not tilted in or out; adjust as needed while the thinset is still wet.

Setting the Backsplash

16 Start the mosaic trim at the most conspicuous end of the vanity. Because the trim pieces fit into each other, you must cut off the projecting portion on the first piece as follows: Rest a trim piece on the counter tile against the wall, aligning the lower edge of the trim with the edge of the counter tile. Insert a spacer under the trim piece near each end. Tape the upper edge of the trim

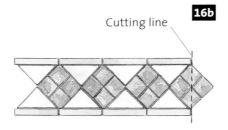

Cutting line

piece to the wall to secure. Using the small carpenter's square, mark a cutting line as shown in the photo and the illustration below left.

17 Lightly mark a line on the wall at the upper edge of the trim piece with a pencil. Lay kraft paper on the counter and adhere masking paper to the wall above the line. Comb thinset vertically onto the wall and set the first trim piece, with spacers underneath. Check the upper edge with the carpenter's level. Insert spacers underneath the lower white ceramic pieces to help keep the trim from sagging.

Turning a Corner

18 To make the backsplash design flow smoothly around a corner, measure from the end of the just-set trim piece to the corner. Subtract the width of the grout line and the thickness of a trim piece to arrive at the cut length of the next trim piece.

19 Measure and mark the trim piece for cutting; double-check your measurement to avoid making a cutting error. Cut the piece on the wet saw; put the leftover piece aside.

20 Comb thinset onto the wall and set the cut piece with spacers underneath; check it with the level along the upper edge and adjust if necessary. Set the leftover piece on the adjoining wall, positioning it away from the corner the same distance as the previous piece. Once the surface and the upper edge are grouted, the design will appear to flow around the corner.

21 Finish setting the backsplash, cutting the final piece as needed.

Grouting and Sealing the Tile

22 If you are setting or resetting a mirror just above the backsplash, do so now (see pages 136 and 137).

23 Apply painter's tape to the J-channel on the mirror or, if there is no mirror, to the wall just above the trim. See Steps 26 through 28 on page 125 to grout and seal the tile. Use a gloved fingertip to work grout into and between the trim pieces. If there is a mirror just above the trim, also apply grout between the lower edge of the J-channel and the trim. Allow the grout and sealer to dry according to the manufacturer's instructions. Remove the tape.

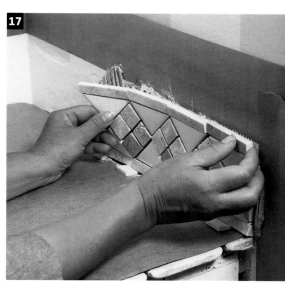

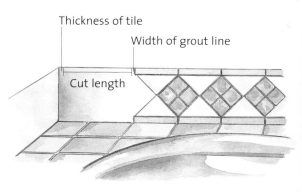

Thickness of tile

Width of grout line

Cut length

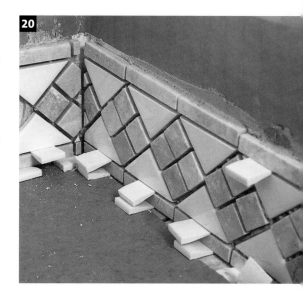

MATERIALS

Knee pads

Steel tape measure

$^{3}/_{8}$-inch particleboard
underlayment
and circular saw*

Pull saw

Staple gun and
18-gauge staples,
1$^{1}/_{4}$ inches long*

Floor leveling compound
and 6-inch putty knife

Pattern paper, rosin
paper, or pattern felt

Utility knife

Masking tape

Carpenter's square with
2-inch-wide legs

Sheet vinyl (see
Resources, page 142)

Pen that will mark vinyl

Vinyl trimming tool
(optional; see Step 14)

Wide brush for cleaning
the vinyl underside

Vinyl adhesive trowel
and vinyl adhesive**

Cotton cloths

Hand roller or rolling pin

Mineral spirits

*See Step 2.

**Use products recom-
mended by the vinyl
manufacturer.

IN A WEEKEND

Vinyl Floor

INSTALLING VINYL FLOORING is within reach of the do-it-yourselfer if the room is small enough to permit a seam-free installation. (See the tip on the facing page.) Some sheet-vinyl manufacturers offer a kit that includes instructions, pattern paper, and helpful tools. Before you commit to this project, however, get an estimate on a professional installation; it may be so reasonable that you'll decide to leave the job to a flooring installer.

T I P

PLAN TO RUN THE VINYL IN THE DIRECTION THAT WILL PREVENT THE NEED FOR SEAMS. IN THIS SMALL BATHROOM, 6-FOOT-WIDE VINYL WAS RUN DOWN THE LENGTH OF THE ROOM FOR A SEAMLESS FIT.

Removing Existing Flooring

1 Remove the baseboards and the existing flooring.

2 If the underlayment (the layer of particleboard on top of the sub-floor) is in excellent condition, leave it in place. If the underlayment is not perfectly smooth, or if it shows signs of water damage, remove it following the appropriate safety guidelines; a flooring supplier can provide you with this information. Clean any debris or old adhesive from the surface of the subfloor.

Making a Sketch

3 Put on the knee pads. Using the steel tape, measure the room. Make a sketch showing the dimensions.

Installing the Underlayment

4 Using your sketch, determine how to install the underlayment with the fewest possible cut pieces.

Measure and mark the pieces; cut them using the circular saw.

5 If necessary, trim door casings with a pull saw to accommodate the underlayment.

6 With the staple gun and the 18-gauge staples, attach the underlayment to the subfloor. Space the staples every 3 inches along the outer edges and the seams. In the interior area, space the staples every 6 inches.

Preparing the Surface

7 Floor leveling compound creates a level surface for the vinyl. Mix the compound according to the manufacturer's instructions. Using the 6-inch putty knife, fill the small depressions at the underlayment seams and any gaps at the edges, such as the small crack between the underlayment and the shower dam shown below.

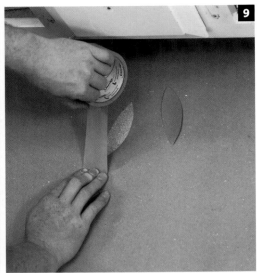

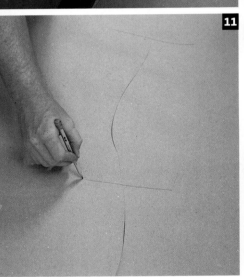

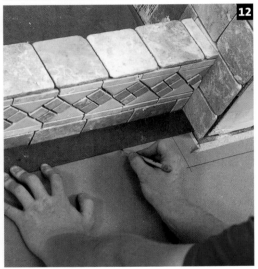

11 Mark lines across the wavy cut every 18 inches so you can align the pieces when you place the pattern on the vinyl for cutting.

12 Make sure the pattern is firmly anchored to the floor through the cutouts. With one leg of the carpenter's square against the wall (or the shower dam, in this photo), mark along the *inner* edge of the leg onto the pattern with a pencil. Work your way around the room to mark the entire pattern, making sure it does not shift. If your heating/cooling register is in the floor, carefully mark the outline on the pattern. Remove the pattern and roll it up.

Marking and Cutting the Vinyl

13 Lay the vinyl faceup on a *clean*, hard surface that's shaded or indoors, such as a smooth patio, deck, or garage floor. (Never lay the vinyl in the sun to mark it for cutting—it

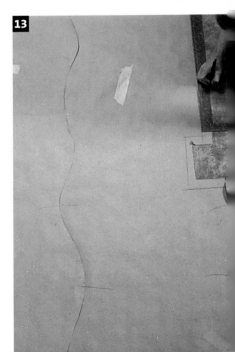

Making the Pattern

8 You will probably need to overlap long pieces of pattern material to get the width you need. Do *not* tape the pieces together; just overlap them down the length of the room. Using the utility knife, cut the material around the perimeter to within 2 inches of the edges. The distance need not be exact, as long as it's less than 2 inches.

9 To keep the pattern from slipping, make small cutouts in the pattern material every 4 feet and anchor the material to the underlayment using the masking tape. Discard the cutouts.

10 Where the pattern pieces overlap down the center, cut a long, wavy line through both layers. Lift the layers and remove the scraps. Lay the pattern pieces down again so they fit together perfectly.

will expand from the heat. If cut when warm, the vinyl will shrink to its original state indoors and the piece will be too small.) Position the pattern on the vinyl, making sure the lines you marked in Step 11 align; anchor the pattern with tape over the cutouts. Align the carpenter's square with the *inner* edge of a leg precisely on the line marked in Step 12. Using the pen, mark the vinyl along the *outer* edge of the leg to create a cutting line. *Make sure you are marking the cutting line correctly or you will ruin the entire sheet of vinyl.*

14 Using the carpenter's square as a straightedge and the utility knife with a fresh blade (or the vinyl trimming tool), cut along the line, through the vinyl. Also cut on the line marked for the heating/cooling register. Be very careful not to cut the surface underneath. (A vinyl trimming tool has a hooked blade on one end that makes it virtually impossible to damage the surface underneath.)

15 With the aid of a helper, turn the vinyl over and clean the underside with the wide brush.

16 Place a scrap of vinyl on the underlayment, up against each door casing. If the vinyl won't slide easily underneath, trim the casing with the pull saw, as shown.

Gluing the Vinyl

17 Vacuum the underlayment thoroughly. Lay out the vinyl on the underlayment to make sure it fits precisely; trim if needed.

18 Pull back the vinyl from the underlayment about halfway and loosely fold it over on itself. Using the adhesive trowel and following the manufacturer's instructions, apply a thin layer of adhesive to the underlayment. Be conservative: the most common mistake is to apply too much adhesive. Use a wet cloth to clean up any excess adhesive.

19 Allow the adhesive to set up according to the manufacturer's instructions. Carefully unfold the vinyl over the adhesive, making sure the piece is perfectly positioned.

20 Working from the just-laid portion of the vinyl, adhere the remainder of the vinyl.

21 Use a hand roller, as shown, or a rolling pin to work out any air bubbles. To clean up dried adhesive, use mineral spirits and a cloth. Avoid walking on the vinyl for 24 hours.

22 If you are planning to paint the walls, do so now. Replace the baseboards.

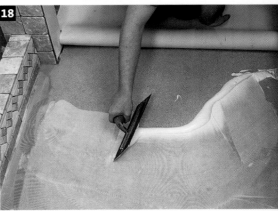

MATERIALS

Standard paint roller with roller cover

2-inch paintbrush

Paint tray with three disposable liners

Latex primer

Off-white latex paint, eggshell finish, for the base coat*

6- by 24-inch acrylic rotary ruler, available at fabric stores and quilt shops

Colored pencil to match the light taupe paint

Carpenter's level

1-inch blue painter's tape

Plastic spackling tool

Small paint roller with roller cover

Light taupe latex paint, eggshell finish, for the stripes*

Pearl-color opalescent paint*

Plastic plate

Heavy plastic wrap

Paper towels

*See Resources, page 142.

IN A WEEKEND

Opalescent Walls

STRIPES PAINTED OFF-WHITE and taupe, then dabbed with pearl-toned paint, created this elegant, understated wall treatment. The project requires no special tools or skills, but you do need to pay careful attention to which stripes you are taping off in Step 6; it's easy to make a mistake. This technique is best suited to smooth walls, but you can still do it if you have textured walls. The opalescent paint will conceal any imperfections in the stripe lines.

3

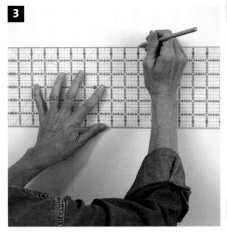

4

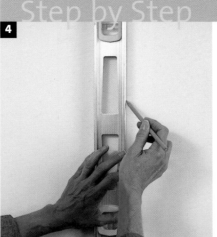

6

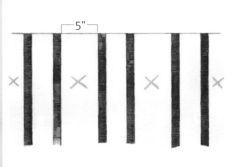

1 Using the standard roller with roller cover and the 2-inch paintbrush, prime the walls with the latex primer. Allow to dry.

2 Apply two coats of the off-white paint, using the brush at the ceiling line, in the corners, and around the trim and the roller to cover the large areas. Allow to dry between coats.

3 Starting in a prominent corner, measure and mark the walls at 5-inch intervals using the rotary ruler and the colored pencil.

4 Draw parallel lines down the wall at the marks you just made, using the carpenter's level to ensure that the lines are plumb.

5 Lightly mark an X with the colored pencil in every other stripe. These will be the stripes you paint light taupe.

6 Tape the stripes in preparation for painting as follows: Place the painter's tape in the blank stripes,

with the edges precisely on the lines. (These stripes will appear narrower than 5 inches because of the tape.) Using the plastic spackling tool, burnish the edges of the tape that are on the lines.

7 Using the small paint roller with roller cover, paint the X-marked stripes light taupe, rolling just over the edges of the tape.

8 When the paint is dry to the touch, gently pull off the tape at a 45-degree angle. Allow to dry thoroughly overnight.

9 Pour approximately ½ cup of the opalescent paint onto the plate. Crumple a piece of the plastic wrap. Dip the wrap into the paint, blot on paper towels, and pounce (dab) the wrap onto the wall, striving for a random effect. Rotate your hand to prevent duplicate patterns. Allow to dry overnight.

7

8

9

Resetting a Mirror

IF YOUR MIRROR RESTS IN A TRACK, you may damage the track when you remove the mirror to do a decorative paint treatment. A glass and mirror store can cut a new track, typically called J-channel, to the required length and file the ends. If you buy the track from a home center, you'll need a metal handsaw and file to do the job yourself. J-channel comes in several finishes; the one shown here is brushed nickel.

MATERIALS

Electric driver/drill with bits

Silver acrylic paint and small paintbrush (optional)

J-channel

Carpenter's level

Stud finder

Blue painter's tape

#6 J-channel screws, 1½ inches long

Package of mirror clips, with screws

1 To remove a mirror, unscrew the mirror holders at the upper edge and, with a helper, carefully lift the mirror out of the track. Unscrew and remove the track. (If you scratch the back of the mirror when you take it out, touch it up with the silver paint.)

2 To reset the mirror, center the J-channel over the vanity at the desired height, with the taller edge against the wall. Use the carpenter's level to make sure the channel is straight, then mark the wall along its upper edge with a pencil. Set the channel aside.

3 Use the stud finder to locate the studs. Mark the studs above where the channel will be with a pencil; mark the studs above where the mirror will be with the blue painter's tape.

4 At each stud, predrill holes through the taller edge of the track and the wall and into the stud. Drill the holes just above the chan-

nel's lower "lip" to make it easy to put in the screws.

5 Attach the track to the wall with the #6 J-channel screws, dimpling the track slightly as shown.

6 With a helper, set the mirror in the track.

7 Hook the mirror clips over the upper edge of the mirror, spacing them to correspond to the location of the studs. With the mirror firmly against the wall, screw the holders into the studs. Remove the tape.

TIP BECAUSE MIRRORS ARE SO HEAVY, IT'S ESSENTIAL TO INSTALL THE SCREWS THROUGH THE J-CHANNEL INTO STUDS, NOT INTO DRYWALL. THE MIRROR CLIPS THAT SLIP OVER THE UPPER EDGE MUST ALSO BE SCREWED INTO STUDS. BE SURE TO CLEAN THE LOWER EDGE OF THE MIRROR BEFORE YOU RESET IT—YOU WON'T WANT TO LIFT IT OUT AGAIN.

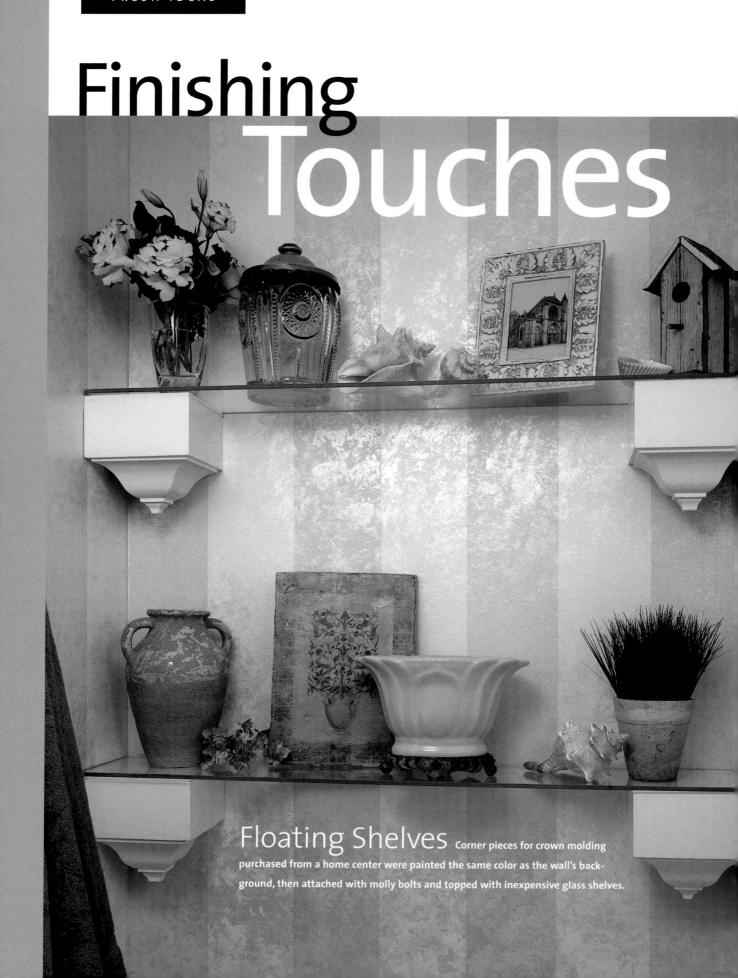

Finishing Touches

Floating Shelves
Corner pieces for crown molding purchased from a home center were painted the same color as the wall's background, then attached with molly bolts and topped with inexpensive glass shelves.

Switch Plate

BELOW: **Painting the switch plate in a continuation of the stripes created a seamless look. To give the plastic surface enough "tooth" to accept the paint, it was first sanded with heavy-grit sandpaper.**

Postcard Picture

ABOVE: **A flea-market frame showcases vintage postcards mounted on leafy handmade paper.**

Molding

ABOVE: **Narrow molding, primed specially for wet areas and painted to match the cabinets, was installed with paneling and molding adhesive.**

Cabinet Knobs

ABOVE: **Solid brass knobs in a stylized leaf design keep to the classic theme and finish off freshly painted cabinets.**

Robe Hooks

BELOW: **Pronged robe hooks are ideally suited to a partial wall. These are brushed nickel, to match the sink faucets.**

Centerset Faucet

LEFT: **A brushed-nickel finish on the faucets (see Resources, page 142) is in sleek contrast to the natural texture of the tumbled stone.**

Shower Fixture
A brushed-nickel shower fixture with chrome accents (see Resources, page 142) reiterates the brushed-nickel hardware on the glass door and the chrome drain cover in the tile floor.

Resources

Many of the tools and products shown in this book are available (or can be special ordered) through a home improvement center. For information on specific products, check with the manufacturers listed below. Web sites change frequently; if you can't find a product on the manufacturer's site, call for assistance. When choosing colors, it's best to go to a store or showroom to see the possibilities. Most web sites can identify the store or dealer nearest you.

Home Centers

Lowe's Home Improvement Warehouse
800-44-LOWES
www.lowes.com
(for store location)

The Home Depot
www.homedepot.com
(for store location)

Products

Country Spa

page 10
Corbels RWC75
Outwater Architectural Products
800-631-8375
www.outwater.com

page 14
Liming wax and finishing wax
Briwax
800-683-6945
www.briwaxusa.com

page 20
Cast-iron grilles
Black Bart Ornamental Iron Works
10481 Gold Flat Rd.
Nevada City, CA 95959
530-265-4816

page 25
Wood appliqués AJ-02323941
Van Dyke's Restorers
800-558-1234
www.vandykes.com

Serene Style

page 28
Wallpaper "Spaced Leaves"
Imperial Home Decor Group
800-539-5399
www.IHDG.com

page 47
Shower fixture, Georgetown series
Price Pfister
800-PFAUCET (732-8238)
www.pricepfister.com

Nantucket Charm

page 48
Wall paint DE 611 "Blue Tease"
Dunn Edwards Paints
888-DE-PAINT (337-2468)
www.dunnedwards.com

page 50
Beadboard panels
Trimac Panel Products
P. O. Box 25277
Portland, OR 97298
503-297-1826

Paint SP 211 "White Heat"
Dunn Edwards Paints
888-DE-PAINT (337-2468)
www.dunnedwards.com

page 54
Commercial VCT,
Imperial Texture series
    51862 "Blue Eyes"
    51863 "Blue Wisp"
Armstrong
800-233-3823
www.armstrong.com

page 58
Shutter
Carriage Trade Shutter Company
1035 42nd St.
Sacramento, CA 95819
916-457-4966

page 61
Cupboard 44212-C
Woodcraft Industries
800-234-5022
www.woodcraftindustries.com

Paint
    DE 144 "Pineapple"
    SP 211 "White Heat"
Dunn Edwards Paints
888-DE-PAINT (337-2468)
www.dunnedwards.com

pages 64 and 65
Sink 5125.080 "Richmond Petite Pedestal Lavatory"
Faucet 3010.008
St. Thomas Creations
619-336-9103
www.stthomascreations.com

Natural Bent

page 70
Lime paint and sealers
Portola Paints & Glazes
818-623-9394
www.portolapaints.com

page 76
Slate flooring tile
Echeguren Slate, Inc.
800-992-0701
www.echeguren.com

page 82
Bar sink 1050.00 "Carlyle Countertop Lavatory"
St. Thomas Creations
619-336-9103
www.stthomascreations.com

pages 82 and 91
Faucet K-11000
"Bol Lavatory Faucet"
Kohler
800–456–4537
www.kohler.com

page 85
Architectural drapery track and
ball-bearing carriers with hooks
800–817–6344
www.kirsch.com

pages 85 and 90
Sheer fabric 8318, color 1
(available through interior
designers only)
Kravet
888–4–KRAVET (457–2838)
www.kravet.com

page 88
Light fixture "MonoRail"
Pendant shades "Midnight"
("High Noon")
Tech Lighting
847–410–4400
www.techlighting.com

page 89
Mirrored cabinet VM130
Zenith Product Corp.
800–892–3986
www.zenith-interiors.com

page 89
Glass curtain
Bedrock Industries
877–283–7625
www.bedrockindustries.com

Color Splash

page 94
Solid-color cotton fabrics
Cherrywood Fabrics, Inc.
888–298–0967
www.cherrywoodfabrics.com

page 96
Swiss Paper 14019 "Turquoise"
Loose Ends
503–390–2348
www.looseends.com

page 98
Jasba ceramic tile, Provence series,
"Moss green, glossy"
Sierra Tile & Stone
530–477–8453

pages 102 and 106
Opaque ¾-inch glass tile
Mosaic Mercantile
877–9–MOSAIC (966–7242)
www.mosaicmercantile.com

Translucent 1-inch glass tile
Marcato Tile Distributors
800–664–0363

Tile adhesive, grout, and tools
Mosaic Mercantile
877–9–MOSAIC (966–7242)
www.mosaicmercantile.com

page 108
Paint
    722 (lighter blue)
    724 (darker blue)
Benjamin Moore Paint
800–344–0400
www.benjaminmoore.com

Classic Appeal

page 114
Glass block, Premiere series, and
Mortar I installation supplies
Pittsburgh Corning
800–624–2120
www.pittsburghcorning.com

pages 120 and 126
Tumbled natural stone
4-inch tile TS01
1-inch sheet-mounted tile TS01
4- by 12-inch mosaic trim FA50

daltile
800–933–TILE (933–8453)
www.daltile.com

page 130
Commercial vinyl sheet,
Perspectives series
    33206 "Painted Bronze"
Armstrong
877–ARMSTRONG (276–7876)
www.armstrong.com

page 134
Paint
    "Super White"
    1037 (Taupe; ask for "half-
    formula")
Benjamin Moore Paint
800–344–0400
www.benjaminmoore.com

Paint, Ovation series,
"Opulence Pearl"
Pratt & Lambert
800–BUY–PRAT (289–7728)
www.prattandlambert.com

pages 140 and 141
Sink faucet and shower fixture,
Georgetown series
Price Pfister
800–PFAUCET (732–8238)
www.pricepfister.com

Tools

Makita
800–4MAKITA (462–5482)
www.makita.com

Senco
800–543–4596
www.senco.com

Index